Fireweed Evangelism

Also by Elizabeth R. Geitz

Entertaining Angels

Gender and the Nicene Creed

Soul Satisfaction

Women's Uncommon Prayers (co-editor)

Recovering Lost Tradition (co-author)

Welcoming the Stranger

Fireweed Evangelism

Christian Hospitality
in a Multi-Faith World

Elizabeth R. Geitz

CHURCH PUBLISHING
New York

A catalog record for this book is available from the Library of Congress.

ISBN 0-89869-459-0

Church Publishing Incorporated
445 Fifth Avenue
New York, NY 10016
www.churchpublishing.org

5 4 3 2 1

Prayerfully dedicated to the
clergy and laity of the Diocese of New Jersey,
who have enriched my ministry beyond measure,
and
To the memory of all those
throughout history who have lost their lives
in acts of terror committed in the name of God

Contents

Blessings

God has blessed me with the support of many caring, courageous colleagues during the writing of *Fireweed Evangelism*. Why courageous? Authoring a book that seeks to deal faithfully with the issue of Christian evangelism, in light of our pluralistic world, has been a challenge. At times I have felt as if I were walking on a tightrope, praying all the while for God to show me a way to the other side. There were times when I fell off, deleted entire pages of manuscript, and started over. How safely I have arrived at the other side will be for you, the reader, to decide.

My deep appreciation goes first of all to Mr. Frank Tedeschi, vice president and executive editor of Church Publishing, who first believed not only in the concept of Fireweed Evangelism, but believed with me that the church needs a new way forward on issues related to evangelism in light of the reality of pluralism today. Ms. Cynthia Shattuck was a dream of an editor, with imaginative suggestions throughout our work together. Getting to know her has been an added blessing. The Rev. Molly Dale Smith, D.Min., shared numerous reference books on evangelism and helpful feedback on the first draft, as did the Rt. Rev. David B. Joslin, the Rev. John Koenig, Ph.D., and the Rev. Alice Downs. The Rev. Dee Dee Turlington, Ph.D., senior pastor of the Westfield Baptist Church, provided much needed support along the way. Her comment that "a lot of my Baptist friends could use this" was most heartening. In addition, I count my blessings often for my bishop, the Rt. Rev. George E. Councell, and my colleagues at Diocesan House, the Rev. Canon Lee Powers and the Rev. Canon Tom Kerr. As in many other projects, their encouragement and insight have been invaluable, especially because we have differing theological perspectives. Those differences are a blessing in many areas of my ministry.

Last and never least is my husband, Michael, who spent hours reading every word of the manuscript, challenging me on sections related to September 11, and in general providing an excellent "view from the pew." I keep telling him I've written my last book, and another one always seems to appear. His love and understanding are a special blessing.

Happy are the people to whom such blessings fall.
Psalm 144:15

Fireweed Evangelism

Introduction

Throughout my years of involvement in hospitality ministry, clergy and lay leaders have repeatedly asked me one question, "Why won't our members reach out and bring others into the church?" Their questions and desperate looks are often followed by one of these statements: "We used to have a welcoming program, but it just fizzled out." "The committed people we do have are overinvolved and burned out." "Our members won't invite anyone to church."

Underlying each of these concerns is one word — motivation. What is the motivation that prompts some Christians ardently to bring others into their faith communities, while others won't engage in evangelism and avoid those who do? Is there any hope that this latter group will one day become enthusiastic evangelists?

As often happens, I stumbled upon an answer to this question long after I had stopped looking for it. Significantly, God led me to it in the immediate wake of September 11, 2001. In the months following the tragedy, I closely examined this disaster which was, in part, the result of exclusivist religious claims, the belief that one religion is the only "right religion"; all others are insufficient or lacking in some way. Was this belief meant to be a part of Christian evangelism, which has historically proclaimed that Jesus is the only way to God; salvation can come only through him? I doubted it, but was not certain, so I embarked on a journey of discovery.

In Part I of *Fireweed Evangelism*, I uncover what I call my "evangelism elephant," my personal history with the word "evangelism" that kept me from pursuing this much-needed ministry. My hesitation was twofold. First, I felt the need to acknowledge the validity of religions other than Christianity; second, I felt a discomfort with conventional evangelistic methods that focused on a pressured need to "save" the other. Naming

3

my reasons freed me to find my particular motivation for bringing others into the church. I name that motivation "Fireweed Evangelism." A fireweed is the first flower to bloom in burned-out places after a catastrophe, bringing abundant, colorful life out of the ashes of death. The experience of new birth lies at the heart of Fireweed Evangelism, which involves one soul reaching out in love to another soul in need of the healing power of the risen Christ. Embodied within this reaching out are a respect for and a willingness to be formed by another's religious experience or faith tradition. The exercises included in this section are to help you discover your own particular motivation, which may or may not be the same as mine.

In Part II the issue of context is addressed. Once you have discovered your motivation for engaging in evangelism, to whom do you reach out and bring into the body of Christ? Where are you likely to find them? As your church begins to grow, it is important to realize that growth alone can actually destabilize a congregation. For that reason, I have included a holistic model for church growth and health, urging readers to focus on their heritage, vision, and moral commitment, as they reach out to bring others into it.

Part III, which draws on and expands material developed in my earlier book *Entertaining Angels*, discusses the biblical basis for hospitality ministry inside the church and a concrete plan for putting it into action. How will you welcome your guests once they arrive? What would make them stay? The uniqueness of Christian hospitality is addressed, as well as the nuts and bolts of newcomer ministry. The forms and handouts needed to establish a vibrant welcoming program in your church are also included.

Fireweed Evangelism thus addresses three critical areas of reaching out and welcoming the stranger into your church community — motivation, context, and action. A focus on one or two without the third can result in an incomplete program that diminishes over time, not meeting the needs of those involved. With a firm understanding of both their motivation and context, more people will become involved in this ministry that is so vital to the health and forward movement of our church.

This book is offered to you with the wisdom gained from eighteen years of public writing and speaking, along with the wonder of a new discovery, recently made. May this combination of the new with the old provide us with an engaging way forward, built upon the past while moving beyond it to address present realities.

The Rev. Canon Elizabeth R. Geitz
Pentecost 2004

Part I

MOTIVATION

I will seek the lost, and I will bring back the strayed,
and I will bind up the injured, and I will strengthen the weak.

– Ezekiel 34:16 –

Chapter 1

Seeing the Elephant

There are times in our lives when God startles us with a long-awaited revelation, one prayed for but since forgotten. Such moments of unexpected insight can lead us to new paths on our ever-twisting spiritual journeys. Where they will ultimately lead us we do not know, yet we embark nonetheless, filled with a sense of adventure and hope. Such a moment occurred for me shortly after the tragedy of September 11, 2001. It was a crisp November day as Clergy Conference 2001 dawned in the Episcopal Diocese of New Jersey. A dynamic evangelism consultant from Tennessee was our speaker, and I was cautiously hopeful. I had often prayed that the ministry of evangelism would come alive for me, but something always seemed to be missing.

As the author of *Entertaining Angels* I have been a keynote speaker on hospitality ministry in numerous dioceses, at our church's national convention, and at gatherings of other denominations. Even so I seldom mentioned evangelism, although I often engaged in it by inviting friends to church. Yes, I was a closet evangelist, and this seeming contradiction confused me. Could our clergy conference begin to unravel this paradox, particularly in the post-9/11 climate of disbelief and pervasive sadness?

On the second afternoon of the conference, our energetic speaker suddenly looked uncharacteristically timid. He ducked his head and said, "I hope I don't offend anyone here, but I need to tell you how I feel about something." He paused and we all sat transfixed in our seats. "I believe that if we are not saved by Jesus Christ, then we are not saved. Jesus is the only way to God. There is no other way. This is my motivation for evangelism. It's what drives me day in and day out to bring others to Christ."

In his openness about his own reasons for participating in evangelism, the belief that Jesus Christ is the one and only way to God, our speaker gave voice to that which is often unspoken. When an obvious, yet significant reality is left unsaid, it can be called "the elephant in the room." For me, the elephant in the evangelism room had finally been named, but no one seemed to notice and the talk resumed. Yet I felt as if the earth had shaken, as if something cataclysmic had occurred. Had my prayers of long ago somehow been answered?

I then found myself reflecting on how sad it was that our speaker felt he had to apologize for believing in this particular view of evangelism. Yet I realized his apology was logical, since many of us in that room, as he instinctively knew, did not live out our faith within his belief system. How many mainline Protestants today believe that Jesus is the only way to God? In *The Heart of Christianity* Marcus Borg refers to a 2002 poll from PBS's *Religion and Ethics Newsweekly* and *U.S. News and World Report*, which found that "only 17 percent of the respondents affirmed the statement, 'My religion is the only true religion.'"[1] I decided long before I attended seminary that my Jewish and Islamic sisters and brothers are not condemned to an eternity of hell and damnation simply because they are not Christian. And what about Buddhists and Hindus? Where do they fit into the grand scheme? Do I believe it is my call as a Christian to convert people of other faiths to my faith to save them from eternal damnation? I did not, I do not, and I doubt that I ever will.

Yet I have an abiding passion for bringing others into the body of Christ. If not to save them from eternal damnation, in what motivation is this passion rooted? Could it provide the link that has been missing from my ministry? Could it possibly be a link for others? The sincerity of our speaker's motivation was clear. There is no doubt in my mind that God does call him, and may call you, to reach out to others in the name of Jesus for the very purpose of winning their souls. He and others who share his belief have carried on the work of evangelism with little help from those of us who do not share their call. For this reason, I owe people with this call a great debt of gratitude.

At one time in my life I fervently prayed for God to fill me with their particular evangelistic fervor. In the mid-1970s, I attended Vanderbilt

University in Nashville, when the Campus Crusade for Christ movement was flourishing. There were white billboards around the city proclaiming, "I found it," in bold black letters. The "it" referred to Jesus or the Holy Spirit, to being born again. But "it" eluded me and I felt left out. Did God not want me? Why wouldn't God give "it" to me?

Some of my dormitory friends were involved in the movement and predictably urged me to join them. I listened to their audiotapes of preachers and prayed and prayed for God to speak to me through them. Why? Because I could see that my friends were filled with a sense of peace that eluded me. I wanted what they had, but did not know how to obtain it. But pray as I might, nothing changed within me. I simply did not respond to the message in the same way they did. Much later in life, I understood that this occurred because God does not speak to all of us in the same way. This is what Paul Jones refers to as people living in different theological worlds. In his book *Theological Worlds: Understanding the Alternative Rhythms of Christian Belief*, Jones writes, "The church of the future must be committed to a pluralism of alternatives, sufficiently viable to touch creatively the individual and social diversity operative in modern life … leading to lively choice between alternative faith-styles." Writing out of this assumption, Jones calls for the Christian church of the future to celebrate the plurality of theologies *within it* and to be "self-consciously variegated."[2]

Within this context we are all free to explore our own understanding of and call to evangelism, but where to start? As soon as the conference was over I turned to my trusted theological dictionary, which offered a helpful beginning point for this new phase of my spiritual journey. "While the New Testament is the basis of the church's understanding of evangelism, it does not describe a model or define a programme for the kind of cross-cultural mission and inter-faith dialogue in which today's evangelists must engage. … The challenge to the contemporary church is how to do evangelism in a pluralistic world, how to be both ecumenical and evangelical at the same time, affirming the truth of other faiths without compromising the uniqueness of Christ."[3]

In making this assertion, it is important to note that Christianity was born in the midst of a pluralistic culture. There were many different faith traditions at that time, as well. So what marks the twenty-first century as different? There are now two thousand years of established Christian history that includes interactions with those of other faiths. While some of those interactions have been positive, some have decidedly not been, as we will see in the next chapter. We must learn from mistakes in the past — both those we have made and those that have been made toward us.

Studying evangelism in the immediate wake of September 11 opened my eyes to the pain that can result from exclusivist religious claims. This truth had always been present, but I had not previously seen it. With this long-awaited revelation before me, I begin my exploration along a new, untested path. Come along with me as I seek a different path for evangelism, one that upholds the uniqueness of Christ without religious exclusivity, a motivation that speaks to the pluralistic world in which we live.

Not only is our world as the global village pluralistic, but so are our local communities. Look around you! God has blessed us with a plurality of faith traditions within the United States; our neighbors whom God has spoken to through a variety of means are all around us. In *A New Religious America,* Harvard professor Diana Eck writes that there are about six million Muslim Americans (as many as all Episcopalians and Presbyterians combined); four million Buddhist Americans (more than either Episcopalians or Presbyterians), and approximately one million Hindus in the United States (about as many as in the United Church of Christ).[4] With such a rich diversity of religious expression in our own country, the opportunities for learning from one another are immense.

The wonderful reality of spiritual journeys is that we never know what God has in mind for us. We simply must trust and follow, realizing that we will encounter curves, bumps, and dead ends along the way. In persevering, however, we are invariably stronger and wiser for the journey. In joining me, keep in mind that God may not lead you down this particular path. God may lead you to another, making our Christian tradition richer for the "self-consciously variegated" perspectives within it.

Chapter 2

Blazing a New Path

Looking Back

Before beginning a journey along any new path, it is helpful to study the history that has led you to it. The attack of September 11 was a turning point for me, shedding light on the tragedy that can result from a belief in religious exclusivism when that belief is taken to the extreme. While exclusivist religious claims are only part of a web of complex political, social, and religious issues that led to the attack, they are a contributing factor and therefore call for examination by people of faith. In questioning this fundamentalist Islamic belief, I must ask about my own faith tradition.

Has a belief in Christianity as the only true religion ever brought similar suffering and tragedy to people of other religions? How might that history inform us as we move forward? While Christian history can be viewed from a variety of valid perspectives, I decided to focus primarily on the work of a multicultural theologian since pluralism lies at the heart of my concern. Many new perspectives can emerge when we are willing to see ourselves through the eyes of the other.

Theologian Raimundo Panikkar has lived in Hindu and Christian, Eastern and Western cultures with doctorates in both philosophy and theology. He writes of five turning points in Christian history — evangelistic witness, conversion, crusade, mission, and dialogue. He is careful to point out that these historical periods often overlap; thus they are not strictly chronological. Nevertheless, Panikkar places evangelistic witness in the first centuries of Christian history up through the death of St. Augustine in 430. Jesus' apostles along with his disciples, some of whom were women, spread the gospel message beyond the borders of Palestine, witnessing to the power of the risen Christ in their lives. Because Christianity threatened the world order, and the Roman emperor in particular, early Christians were often martyred for their beliefs. Legend has it that each apostle died the death of a martyr, with Peter being crucified upside down. Likewise, many of their followers were not spared an untimely death. "They were martyrs," Panikkar writes, "witnesses to an event."[1]

A period of conversion then followed, as Christianity became the official religion of the Roman Empire. Not only being a member of the official religion was necessary, but also a change of heart was needed, a conversion to Christ. Entire countries were converted to Christianity, particularly the peoples of Europe. This lasted until the Middle Ages and the establishment of Christianity throughout Europe. From the eighth century to well past the fall of Constantinople in 1453, according to Panikkar, the dominant force in shaping Christian consciousness was the threat from Islam. At this point, Christians became soldiers, crusaders, which strongly influenced the church's self-understanding.

Scholar Bernard Lewis echoes Panikkar's view in *What Went Wrong? Western Impact and Middle Eastern Response.* He writes, "For most medieval Muslims, Christendom meant, primarily, the Byzantine Empire, which gradually became smaller and weaker until its final disappearance with the Turkish conquest of Constantinople in 1453."[2] Thus, Islam was the dominant world religion at the time, not Christianity. As I read these accounts of fifteenth-century Christendom, I realize that even ten years ago I would have been surprised to learn of the historical dominance of Islam; I simply was not aware of it. That is why educating ourselves about the past, particularly in regard to the three Abrahamic faiths — Judaism, Christianity, and Islam — is a critical part of finding a new path for the future.

Panikkar goes on to state that Christian crusades evolved into almost annual expeditions characterized at times by extreme brutality, both toward the Jews at home and the subjected peoples of the East. It is at this unfortunate point in Christian history that the belief in Christianity as the only true religion intensified. All others were deemed to be false. This belief in the exclusive claim of Christianity, furthermore, inevitably led into a fourth period, one that Panikkar characterizes as mission. He writes that when Columbus came to America in 1492, the Indians who inhabited the land could not be considered a threat, as were the Muslims in earlier centuries. Nevertheless, the European desire to conquer was still strong. At this point, Christians became missionaries rather than crusaders, evangelizing the Indians that they might turn from their pagan ways and accept a Christian belief system and way of life.

With a belief in the superiority of Christianity over all other religions, missionary work was extended to the far reaches of the globe, first by Europeans to America and then from America to numerous third world countries. In *God Has Many Names,* theologian John Hick reminds us that this missionary work was based on a belief in the thirteenth-century Roman Catholic doctrine *Extra ecclesiam nulla salus* (Outside the church, no salvation), with its nineteenth-century Protestant missionary equivalent (Outside Christianity, no salvation).[3] Twentieth-century theologian Karl Barth also articulates this view in relation to mission work. In *Church Dogmatics* he writes that Christianity "alone has the commission and authority to be a missionary religion, i.e., to confront the world of religion as the one true religion, with absolute self-confidence to invite and challenge it to abandon its ways and to start on the Christian way."[4]

As Christians increasingly interacted with those of other faith traditions, they began to sense the value inherent in some of them; theological reflection began. In the midst of these reflections came two world wars and the deaths of millions of innocent people. Some Christians gradually began to realize that they could no longer evangelize people in other countries. It is at this point that the contemporary age was born, with its far different focus in missionary work.

As I studied Panikkar's perspective on my faith tradition, I began to wonder if Christianity were unique in believing in the exclusivity and superiority of its own tradition. Professor Seyyed Hossein Nasr, a world-renowned Islamic philosopher and author of *The Heart of Islam: Enduring Values for Humanity,* states that all three Abrahamic faiths have historically believed they were the only true religion. He explains that this was the normal human situation for thousands of years, in part because people were not exposed to religions outside their own village. Therefore, he cautions against criticizing these beliefs simply because they no longer work in today's world of the global village.

Believing that one's own faith is the only true faith, in itself, is not necessarily problematic. It is the actions undertaken as a result of these beliefs that have caused untold human suffering both in the past and present. A study of all religious traditions worldwide shows that almost every tradition contains a history of the harmful effect of religious absolutism resulting in sanctified violent aggression, exploitation, and intolerance.[5] It is this part of Christian history that must not be repeated as we move forward. It is for this reason that I seek a different path.

Fortunately, Panikkar's view of the present age of Christendom is more positive. The last period he discusses is characterized by dialogue. Colonial political order has been dismantled, while technology has changed the world into a global village with worldwide communication readily available. "Many Christians," he writes, "no longer want to conquer, not even to convert; they want to serve and to learn; they offer themselves as sincere participants in an open dialogue."[6] At this time, the model of the Servant Church emerges in both mainline Protestantism and Catholicism, and Jewish-Christian dialogue becomes common. The 1988 Lambeth Conference commended a document called *Jews, Christians and Muslims: The Way of Dialogue* to churches within the Anglican Communion. It was not, however, until the tragedy of September 11, 2001, that such dialogue occurred on a widespread basis. There seems to be a sincere desire on the part of Christians to learn about other faiths, to truly understand them. Hospitality in the sense of mutual respect for another's tradition begins to emerge. We can begin to look forward to a new era.

Looking Ahead

Blazing a new path, regardless of where it ends, can begin only with a solid foundation of mutual respect. To enable such respect to grow requires an intentional process of praying together, then listening and learning from each other. Since Christianity itself was partially shaped by dialogue with other faith traditions, the process of listening, learning, and allowing new understandings to emerge is an important part of our tradition on which we can now build. In his 1998 report to the Lambeth Conference of the Anglican Communion Michael Nazir-Ali writes, "The Christian faith was born in a plural environment, and had to relate not only to Judaism and to 'classical' Graeco-Roman religion but also to the various 'mystery' cults of the Mediterranean world as well as state religions such as Zoroastrianism in the Persian Empire."[7] Christianity came to be deeply influenced by a number of these traditions.

As we reach out in hospitality to our sisters and brothers of different faith traditions, prayer must lie at the center of our actions. Frank T. Griswold, presiding bishop of the Episcopal Church, wrote the following prayer in the fall of 2000, which was posted on the church's website:

> That the people who live in the Holy Land and confess the three Abrahamic faiths — Judaism, Christianity, and Islam — will find a way to live together with mutual trust, we join our prayers with the prayers of Jews, Christians, and Muslims, praying for a genuine and abiding peace in the Holy Land, and for the presence of God's unfailing love with those who have suffered through this conflict over the last decades.

Prayer that lifts up the three faiths in unity can only help facilitate dialogue and understanding between these faith traditions. In addition, when Christians recite the Nicene Creed, it is important to be aware that the beginning phrase, "We believe in one God," applies to our Jewish and Islamic sisters and brothers as well and unites us to them, for all three faiths believe in the same God, the God of Abraham.

Christians can enter into dialogue with people of other faith traditions in a number of ways. We do not need to wait for an offering that features well-known leaders of different religious traditions. Rather, it is possible to engage in such dialogue in our everyday lives. As Bishop Nazir-Ali goes on to say in the Lambeth report cited above, "Dialogue happens when people who are neighbours or colleagues begin to talk to each other about their beliefs and spiritual experience. It can happen when people join together to struggle for freedom or human rights and discover that they are doing so because of their faith." In entering into dialogue with people of other faith traditions today, Christians may be changed; indeed mutual transformation may occur. How this might change the history of Christian thought is yet to be seen. For individual Christians, however, it has already led to a variety of perspectives, including the positions of exclusivism, inclusivism, and pluralism.[8]

In *Revisioning the Church,* contemporary theologian Peter C. Hodgson expresses what is called the pluralist position by positing "that the great world religions have equally valid claims and that each is culturally relative."[9] Adherents of this perspective hold that people of different faiths can all find salvation within their own faith tradition. Anglican bishop Michael Ingham of Canada echoes this sentiment in *Mansions of the Spirit: The Gospel in a Multi-Faith World.* If Christians believe that

> the growth of God-consciousness need not end with Jewish-Christians of the first century, that a new understanding is possible and indeed necessary for world peace and survival, then we may feel ourselves impelled towards a yet wider view of God's self-disclosure.... It would not deny the central witness of Scripture to a universally sovereign Lord whose will it is that all people should be saved, but rather take that witness to its next logical step.... Divine grace may be experienced through other religious paths without any contradiction of the way of salvation offered in Jesus Christ.[10]

While a pluralist view may be appealing, especially in light of recent history, it has led some theologians to abandon claims to the validity of the doctrine of the Incarnation (the belief that Jesus is the Son of God) and of the Trinity (the belief that God is three in One). Since I personally cannot justify such a radical departure from my faith tradition, this particular path is not one that I am comfortable following. My journey continues.

In *Jesus and the Other Names,* contemporary theologian Paul F. Knitter acknowledges the validity of the Incarnation and the Trinity while still holding that other religions can also possess valid truth claims. He writes, "Jesus' good news *defines* God, but it does not *confine* God; it reveals what Christians feel is *essential* to a true knowledge of the Divine, but it does not provide *all* that makes up such knowledge." Significantly, this position is echoed in a 1989 statement issued by the World Council of Churches: "We cannot point to any other way of salvation than Jesus Christ; at the same time we cannot set limits to the saving power of God." These perspectives, while upholding the uniqueness of the Christian claim, encourage dialogue as a way to learn more of the divine than can be gleaned from a purely Christian point of view. This approach is also similar to "the Fourth Option," or dialogue, initially articulated by Canadian theologian David Lochhead in 1988.[11]

The concept that Christianity, as well as all other faith traditions, can be enriched by dialogue with one another addresses the needs of our pluralistic world while not abandoning the uniqueness of Christianity. Not only do we need a better understanding of one another to survive in our world today, without such understanding we will all lose the richness that can come from learning about another's religious belief system. Rather than viewing one another as competitors in an ultimate test of who is right and who is wrong, as has historically been the case, we could view each other as fellow travelers from which to learn something of the divine that perhaps we ourselves did not yet know.

The image of one mountain with many paths is an instructive one. Rather than being in competition with one another, one might imagine a crossing over to walk along another's path at some point, befriending the person on his or her spiritual journey, learning from that person's experience, which has of necessity been different from one's own. Perhaps there is an invitation to another to walk along one's own path for a while, learning and conversing along the way. Each could then return to his or her own traditional path, enriched and wiser for the journey. Is there a concern that one might stay forever on the other's path? Yes, but that possibility is open to all travelers and is a chance that may well be worth taking, given the alternatives.

Such walking along another's spiritual path has been occurring for a number of years within Eastern and Western monasteries, with few of us outside those structures being aware of it. In *By Faith and Hospitality: The Monastic Tradition as a Model for Interreligious Encounter*, Pierre-François de Bethune, O.S.B., writes of the hospitality of Catholic monks to monks of other faith traditions as a rich environment for interfaith dialogue. In doing so, however, he is careful to distinguish between hospitality and dialogue:

> Dialogue belongs to the realm of *logos*, where communication is made through language.... Hospitality belongs to the realm of *ethos*, which consists in letting the other in, of ourselves entering the other's space. Communication is made by gestures, less explicit than language but also less ambiguous.... Hospitality acts as an environment for dialogue.

Within this environment, Buddhist and Christian monks in particular have prayed together, using their common spiritual struggle to unite with the divine, to unite them to one another. The experience of communal prayer has led to a mutual respect and understanding of each other's traditions. "Prayer," Bethune writes, "is indeed the shortest route between two people. When two people pray, God is not a third: he is the First, welcoming the one and the other."[12]

The belief that other religions can also hold valid truth claims that are instructive for Christians feels quite natural to me given my particular history and understanding of God. However, for those who may not feel comfortable with this perspective, a suggestion from Benedictine spirituality might be helpful. In her preface to *Living with Contradiction: An Introduction to Benedictine Spirituality*, Anglican writer Esther de Waal states:

> At the heart of the Gospel, as at the heart of Christ's own life, of course there is paradox. So living with the Rule of St. Benedict means living with paradox, with contradiction.... I shall go on until the day of my death trying to hold differing things together.... Today as I look around me I see a world in which there is not so much holding together as splitting apart.... How far this is from the stance of St. Benedict, whose first, opening word of the Rule establishes the keynote of all that is to follow: *Listen.*[13]

If we listen lovingly to others with the ear of the heart, as St. Benedict's Rule goes on to suggest, and hold seemingly conflicting viewpoints together in creative tension, it becomes more difficult to make claims of religious exclusivism. The same is true if we begin by praying deeply with one another. From these vantage points, true hospitality can be extended, which always involves an emptying of the self and a reaching out to the other with a willingness to risk being transformed by the encounter. To not do so results in a cutting off from the other, an isolation that can lead to claims of exclusivity.

Archbishop Rowan Williams once spoke of the Benedictine Rule in a sermon, "We tend, all of us, to try to solve our problems by more talking, and less listening. As you read the Rule of St. Benedict, what you see being defined before you is a method for creating a listening community. And not simply a community of people who are all listening to the same thing...but a community of people who are listening intently to each other." This kind of Benedictine "listening" took place at a conference at Drew University in Madison, New Jersey, on September 11, 2002, called "Is There a Future for Religious Pluralism?" Representatives of the three Abrahamic faiths gave meditations and keynote addresses. What can we, as Christians, learn from our Jewish and Islamic sisters and brothers?

Rabbi William Horn illuminated a Jewish belief that it is possible for people to disagree and both be right. "Does it have to make sense?" he then asked, in a rabbinic mode of address. "No. It just has to make sense to God." I have thought of his words often since the conference, particularly when I have disagreed with someone. How liberating this insight is, not only in dialogue with people of other religions, but also in everyday life.

In a similar vein, Dr. Ali Chaudry, a Muslim, led us in a meditation on these words of the Koran: "To you, your way. To me mine." How different history would be if all three of our faiths had regularly prayed together and listened to one another lovingly with the "ear of the heart." How different history would be if all three had lived according to a dialogical understanding of God's will for the world rather than one based on claims of absolutism.

As we pray together and listen with the "ear of the heart" to other faith traditions, acknowledging their specific truth claims, where does that leave us as Christian evangelists? I cannot answer that question for you, but for me it leads toward developing an understanding of evangelism undergirded by prayer and based on dialogue that upholds the uniqueness of Christ.

Is this possible?

Chapter 3

Fireweed Evangelism

In witnessing to the central role of Jesus Christ in our lives, we can only speak for ourselves. None of us can state with authenticity what other people have experienced, either within the Christian tradition or outside it. What we can witness to is our own experience. In the words of the familiar hymn, we can "tell the old, old story of Jesus and His love." How we do that will depend primarily on the theological world we inhabit.

In *Theological Worlds,* Paul Jones writes that this process of talking about God, or theologizing, is "more complex than usually assumed, since it is thoroughly sociocultural and thoroughly autobiographical."[1] As a result, the universal story of Jesus and his love will not and cannot be the same for everyone. For example, you might view yourself primarily as a forgiven sinner. Jesus is the One who willingly died to save you from eternal damnation. With Jesus, you too are raised from the dead, both figuratively here on earth and literally at death. There are several passages in the Gospel of John that highlight this perspective. Jesus says: "No one comes to the Father except through me" (14:6), and "whoever has seen me has seen the Father" (14:9). Similarly, the Acts of the Apostles states, "There is salvation in no one else, for there is no other name under heaven given among mortals by which we must be saved" (4:12).

Christians with another view of the world may see themselves primarily as those who have been wounded, but have now been healed through the wounds and love of Jesus and the power of his resurrection. Through Christ's wounds they are healed and with him, they too are raised from the dead — both from the death and numbness of pain here on earth and from a death after life in which there is no union with God.

The first worldview is what motivated the evangelistic efforts of our clergy conference speaker in the Diocese of New Jersey. At its heart is the theology of saving others from their sins through the resurrection of Jesus Christ. In other words, if people accept Jesus Christ as their Savior they are "born again" or "saved." If they do not, they are not saved.

God never spoke to me in this way. Instead, God spoke to me through personal life experiences and my ministry. When I was in my late thirties, my mother took her own life, hurtling me into the depths of a woundedness I could never have imagined. As is often the case when we feel deeply injured, there was a difference between my head and my heart. In my head, I knew that my mother loved our family, and me, very deeply. In many ways, we were the center of her life. Yet in my heart, I felt a sense of rejection that took years to move beyond. My heart said, "Didn't I matter enough to my mother that she would want to live?" "How could she abandon us of her own free will?"

My head knew that for many years she had suffered from clinical depression from which she could find no relief. Yet my heart was the heart of a child who felt betrayed, abandoned, and hurt beyond all reason, even though I was thirty-seven at the time of her death. My head knew that my mother had sinned against no one but perhaps herself. Yet my heart felt that I had been sinned against, if sin is defined as that which deeply hurts another, whether intentional or not.

Into the midst of this woundedness, Jesus came into my life, sat beside me, held me, and did not let me go. At the same time, I knew that he was also sitting beside my mother, holding her and loving her deeply. It is this dual reality that lies at the heart of the paschal mystery, where the cross and resurrection become enveloped in a seamless and selfless act of new birth and new life. The pain is there, but so are the hope and the joy. At the center of these conflicting feelings lies our willingness to be vulnerable, for until we allow ourselves to become vulnerable and feel our pain, new birth cannot occur. The ultimate vulnerability of Christ on the cross shows us the way.

Frederick Buechner relates a similar experience of new life in his short story "The Dwarves in the Stable." Writing of his father's suicide, which took place when he was ten years old, Buechner evocatively describes the movement from woundedness to wisdom:

Even the saddest things can become, once we have made peace with them, a source of wisdom and strength for the journey that still lies ahead. It is through memory that we are able to reclaim much of our lives that we have long since written off by finding that in everything that has happened to us over the years God was offering us possibilities of new life and healing which, though we may have missed them at the time, we can still choose and be brought to life by and be healed by all these years later.[2]

Yes, that which makes us most vulnerable can indeed make us the strongest and that which is most painful in our own lives can enable us to be a source of strength for others.

Through Christ's wounds I was blessedly healed and with him I was figuratively raised from the dead. I accepted Jesus as my Savior not primarily because I had sinned (even though we all do), but because I felt I had been sinned against. This is not the classic Christian theology of salvation, but it has been my theological experience. Is there a part of your autobiography that informs your view of God, your theology? It does not have to be one major event; it may be a series of small experiences that have gradually shaped you over the years. Could this have an impact on a possible call to bring others into the church?

As I continued to reflect on my own experience, to my delight I discovered a scholar who speaks to it and expands upon it. Korean Methodist theologian Andrew Sung Park articulates a similar understanding of salvation in *The Wounded Heart of God: The Asian Concept of Han and the Christian Doctrine of Sin.* To understand his perspective, I first had to understand the Asian concept of *han.*

> Throughout its history, the church has been concerned with the sin of people, but has largely overlooked an important factor in human evil; the pain of the *victims* of sin. . . . Such an experience of pain is called *han* in the Far East. Han can be defined as the critical wound of the heart generated by unjust psychosomatic repression, as well as by social, political, economic, and cultural oppression. . . . Han reverberates in the souls of survivors of the Holocaust, Palestinians in the occupied territories, victims of racial discrimination, battered wives . . . the victims of child-molestation . . . and exploited workers.

To Park's list one might add survivors of September 11, survivors of the wars in Iraq, people whose loved ones commit suicide, and those discriminated against due to their sexual orientation, to name but a few. Historically, the Christian doctrine of sin has not dealt with these groups of people. Instead, "the problems of the victims of sin have been relegated to pastoral counseling. . . . The issue of victims has not been taken seriously at the level of theological doctrine." Park goes on to write that sin and *han* are complementary doctrines, rather than exclusive of one another. "The doctrine of sin can be complemented by the doctrine of *han;* the doctrine of repentance by the doctrine of victim's forgivingness."[3]

For example, if a person is unable to forgive and is therefore locked into a posture of anger, it can get in the way of his or her relationship with God. It can keep God at arm's length, imprisoning the person in bitterness and anger. A doctrine of salvation in which forgiveness is just as important as repentance could reach a greater number of people. The person experiencing *han,* a critical wound of the heart, who needs to forgive can be healed through the wounds of Christ and experience new birth with him through the resurrection. The person who needs to repent can likewise be saved through the death and resurrection of Christ.

In Park's view sin and *han* can be held together in order to have an inclusive view of salvation, one that includes an entry point for both sinner and sinned against. While we are all sinners and all sinned against at different times in our lives, to reach the largest number of people, perhaps the church needs an understanding of salvation that takes both into account. Is there biblical justification for such a dual understanding?

Both views of salvation are poignantly and succinctly held together in 1 Peter. "He himself bore our sins in his body on the cross, so that, free from sins, we might live for righteousness; by his wounds you have been healed" (1 Pet. 2:24). A more inclusive view of salvation could incorporate both perspectives; both could be used effectively in evangelism.

This alternative motivation for evangelism is based on numerous biblical sayings beginning in the Hebrew Scriptures, moving to Jesus' life and teachings, culminating in the cross and resurrection. In Ezekiel, for example, the Lord God says, "I will seek the lost, and I will bring back the strayed, and I will bind up the injured, and I will strengthen the weak" (Ezek. 34:16). In the Gospel of Matthew Jesus tells us: "Come to me, all you that are weary and are carrying heavy burdens, and I will give you rest" (Matt. 11:28). The cross as the manifestation of Jesus' vulnerability or weakness is repeatedly articulated by St. Paul. "For he was crucified in weakness, but lives by the power of God" (2 Cor. 13:4). For this reason, St. Paul speaks of his own power as being "made perfect in weakness" (2 Cor. 12:9). Of the resurrection he writes, "So it is with the resurrection of the dead. What is sown is perishable, what is raised is imperishable.... It is sown in weakness, it is raised in power" (1 Cor. 15:42–43).

Henri Nouwen's classic book *The Wounded Healer* describes the central aspect of woundedness in the healing ministry of the church. Could a similar understanding be incorporated into evangelism? The identification of our own vulnerability with that of Jesus on the cross might enable a Christian to say, "Hurting? Wounded? Come to church with me and I'll introduce you to someone who's 'been there done that' and overcome it — Jesus Christ. By his wounds you will be healed. By his wounds you will be saved and raised from the dead. You are not alone; come with me. New life in the risen Christ is waiting for you."

Those who feel called to engage in evangelism from this vantage point, however, will want to give careful consideration to our own spiritual journey. As Nouwen succinctly states, "Open wounds stink and do not heal." In other words if we have not had a chance to work through our own woundedness and heal, we will be of little help to anyone else, either as a pastoral caregiver or as an evangelist. Nouwen writes:

> When we want to put our wounded selves in the service of others, we must consider the relationship between our professional and personal lives. On the one hand, no minister can keep his own experience of life hidden from those he wants to help. Nor should he want to keep it hidden.... On the other hand, it would be very easy to misuse the concept of the wounded healer by defending a form of spiritual exhibitionism.... This spiritual exhibitionism adds little faith to little faith and creates narrow-mindedness instead of new perspectives.[4]

While Nouwen is writing about these dangers primarily for professionals, the same holds true for lay ministers.

This kind of honesty in the pastoral relationship, however, can be life-giving to others, opening doors to invite them in. This is hospitality at its finest, one Christian soul reaching out to another to share what has been of value within the Christian experience. How do we know we have reached the state of spiritual health that enables us to begin this ministry? By talking with others in our Christian community — our clergy, our spiritual directors, our friends in Christ. Very few of us can be objective about ourselves; in fact, probably none of us can. Before engaging in this or any other ministry, we need to be open to hearing God's word for us through the other. It may not always be what we want to hear. It may not be in keeping with our view of ourselves, but I have found that there is no substitute for listening with an open heart to those whom we trust.

For example, those seeking Holy Orders in most mainline denominations must first work with a church committee on ministry to explore their call. Such committees probe the answers to numerous questions, including, "Are these persons experiencing a call from God, or are their own needs getting in the way? Do they hear God's voice or their own?" Such discernment is not only helpful to those seeking ordained ministry, but to everyone, both lay and ordained who would minister in the name of Christ.

To give yourself a sense of where you are on your journey, you might ask yourself these questions. Do you view yourself primarily as a victim or as a survivor of your experience? Are you filled with feelings of hopelessness, helplessness, anger, or have you come to a place of peace? Are you angry with the other person, with God, with Jesus or have you moved beyond that?

It is vital to address these questions honestly and with the help of those you trust, for I am not advocating evangelism by victims but by survivors. Evangelism by victims involves one wounded soul in need of healing reaching out to bring into the church another wounded soul also in need of healing. When this occurs, I have often seen the individuals who are reaching out actually become a burden to the one they seek to help. As a result, no one is helped. However, when survivors engage in evangelism, the ones reaching out have experienced the healing power of Christ and have had time to move beyond their pain, sorrow, or anger to a place where they can be an agent of healing for another. The wonderful reality of bringing people into the church from this perspective is that with the help and grace of God and the Christian community, the person who is invited can also move from victim to survivor, empowered and strengthened by the healing grace of the risen Christ.

Fireweed Evangelism

I have named this method of bringing people into the church Fireweed Evangelism. A fireweed is a flowering plant that grows best in burnt-over ground. Springing up quickly in areas that have been destroyed by fire, the fireweed flower is the color of pink magenta. After the London Blitz of World War II, fireweed could be seen blooming throughout the ruins of bombed and burnt-over areas of the city. The fireweed, which brings new life to lifeless areas, could be called a resurrection plant and is therefore an apt metaphor for this evangelistic path. Additionally, it connotes strength and perseverance against the odds, as well as the fire of the Holy Spirit, which is the underlying force behind all evangelistic efforts.

What does Fireweed Evangelism look like? One person, healed through the power of the risen Christ, inviting someone to church who also needs Christ's healing touch, without asserting that this is the only path to healing or to God. Central to Fireweed Evangelism is an appreciation of other religious traditions and the understanding that while it begins with vulnerability it ends with new life, new hope. Thus, the paschal mystery lies at its heart, as does the act of baptism. In baptism, Christians are grafted into the body of Christ. Through it, we literally die and rise again with Jesus.

One afternoon my family and I were floating down the Delaware River in a canoe, enjoying the scenery and the solitude of the river. As we rounded a bend, we were suddenly almost on top of a crowd of people standing waist deep in the water, all dressed in white, singing hymns. In the center of the circle, a minister was dunking a woman way under the water three times and bringing her slowly up as he repeated, "I baptize you in the name of the Father and of the Son and of the Holy Spirit." I am sure by the end of her baptism, this woman felt as if she had almost "died" under the water, before literally rising again with Christ. The meaning of baptism was most likely not lost on her! Those of us whose faiths participate primarily in infant baptism, with water being poured over the head, can lose the sense of dying with Christ in the act of baptism itself. Yet the willingness to be vulnerable lies at the heart of baptism just as it lies at the heart of crucifixion.

Fireweed Evangelism, which has at its heart the paschal mystery of dying and rising again with Christ, provides the vantage point from which God calls me to evangelize. This is why I invite people to church, and, as I have shared, it is based in part on autobiography. What about you? Does your life story provide clues for why the church is meaningful to you? Could it provide a reason for bringing others into the church as well?

After discovering a possible motivation, we need to ask ourselves if it upholds the uniqueness of Christianity. Fireweed Evangelism meets this criterion, for it is only the Christian faith that has at its center a crucified and risen Savior. Only Christians can invite someone into their faith community for this reason. This is part of the uniqueness of what we have to offer our world.

Not only individuals but whole communities and groups of people have a story to tell that will affect how they evangelize. In exploring the concept of Fireweed Evangelism further, I find that I have both personal and global reasons for embracing it. We are all affected by events around us, sometimes drastically. Anyone who has ever fought in a war cannot help but be changed dramatically by the experience. The same is true of people who have lived through natural disasters such as earthquakes, hurricanes, fires, or floods. Similarly, people who lived through the Great Depression in America often have a very different outlook on life from those who have never faced such hardship. There are numerous defining, historical events in our lives that affect our autobiographies.

I will never forget the morning of September 11, 2001. As the Canon for Ministry Development and Deployment in the Diocese of New Jersey, I was involved in three days of anti-racism training for our diocesan staff. In the midst of the morning session, our seventy-year-old volunteer receptionist knocked on the door of the meeting room. Her instructions had been to disturb us only in the event of an emergency. "A plane has hit one of the World Trade Centers," she stated in a quivering voice. We were concerned but, like many people, assumed that it was only a small Cessna that had gone off course. Our training continued.

A half hour later, she knocked again. "Another plane has hit the towers, and they think it might be terrorists." We thought she must be overreacting; terrorists don't strike America. The training continued, but I became worried. My husband, Michael, has worked in the World Financial Center directly across from the World Trade Center for over twenty years. I left the room immediately and tried to call him on my cell phone, but all I received was a recording stating that all circuits were busy.

"It's really serious. It really is!" the receptionist pleaded. At that point the training finally stopped. As I continued in vain to get through on the cell phone, I realized something was terribly wrong and went into an adjacent building to listen to the radio. As I kept pushing the redial button on my phone, I heard the reporter on the radio announce that the towers were collapsing at that very moment. I don't believe I have ever felt as helpless or as fearful in my life. A sense of the surreal surrounded me.

Over an hour later, I finally reached my husband. Tears began to stream down my face as I heard Michael's voice. He was in midtown Manhattan for a meeting. He was safe. He was all right. Thanks be to God. Thanks be to God, was all I could think. Michael was unable to leave New York City that day due to tunnel and bridge closings. He spent the night in the midtown hotel where his meeting had been held. On the phone that night he described a scene out of the movie *Independence Day*. All the streets were deserted. No police or emergency workers were in sight, and thick billows of smoke were rising in the distance from what had been the Trade Center Towers. When he walked outside, his eyes and throat burned; the smoke created a thick fog.

Would the nearby Empire State Building be the next target? Would the tunnels or bridges be next? Was it safe to take the train? Needless to say, neither of us slept much that night. With these questions still unanswered, Michael took the train home the next morning. What relief I felt when I finally saw him!

"What can I do to help you?" I blurted out. "I'll do anything. What can I do?"

"Invite everyone in my group over for dinner with their families," he immediately replied. "I just want to see them. I want to count fingers and toes." His answer surprised me, but I was more than eager to comply.

The next thing I knew we were making hamburgers and hot dogs for twenty-eight people in the midst of a complete state of unreality.

The look from the eyes of our friends and colleagues that evening is something that will stay with me forever. These men and women of Wall Street, who make decisions of far-reaching consequences daily, had been rattled to the core. Some had literally run for their lives and seen people jump (and land). Their spouses were comforting friends whose loved ones never made it home. As horrifying as the stories were, there was comfort for us in all being together.

Then it came time to eat. As a priest, I had always secretly hoped that I would be asked to say the blessing at a business dinner. It had never happened. That evening I looked around the group; some were Jewish and some could have been Muslim. I did not know so I asked. There were no Muslims, but in asking I made it very clear that if there had been, everyone was welcome at the table; everyone had a place. Standing on the patio steps with smoke from the Trade Center rising in the background, I said more clearly than perhaps I had said anything in the last twenty-four hours, "You know, we all have the same God. We need to remember that." Then I finally got to say the blessing — for all of us, for our friends who were still missing, for our country, for the food we were about to eat. It was certainly not the way I ever hoped the blessing would occur, but there we were, all united in prayer in powerful, life-giving ways.

Our patio prayer time was but one of hundreds in our country in the days and weeks that followed. Firefighters, police officers, and their families and friends joined hands in prayer as they mourned the missing and dead among them. Black and white, Hispanic and Asian, young and old, straight and gay, poor and wealthy, all reached out to one another with genuine love and concern. Strangers began speaking to each other in New York City with an outpouring of care unlike anything anyone had ever experienced. People were united in their collective pain and woundedness in ways that upheld and supported them all.

What does this have to do with evangelism? For me, it has everything to do with it. Out of great tragedy come great wounds. One way to heal the wounds of our souls, of our nation, is through the wounds of Christ. Yes, people can and do find healing in other faith traditions, but Christianity is unique in what we have to offer, for our Savior has been wounded, as have we; his wounds can heal ours leading us to new life, freeing us from bondage that separates us from the love of God. Why not focus on this central aspect of our Christian faith in order to bring others to it?

Dean Ward Ewing of the General Theological Seminary in New York City tells the story of a fire truck pulling up in front of the seminary on October 10. The captain got out, came up to the reception desk, and asked to speak with someone in charge. The dean was meeting with a professor at the time, who went out to the lobby to greet the captain. "We lost five of our men at the World Trade Center September 11," he said. "This weekend we've invited their families and friends, friends from the neighborhood, and others who have supported us over the last month to come by the firehouse. We will eat together; we will tell stories of their lives and our lives. I've come to ask if there is a priest here who is free on Sunday afternoon and could join us and begin the gathering with some prayers."

I wonder how many times that same fire truck had passed the seminary without anyone ever thinking of going inside. I also wonder how many clergy and seminarians had passed the firehouse without ever thinking of stopping in there.

The experience of living through September 11 has changed forever my view of appropriate evangelistic methods. On that fateful day, the exclusivist claim of the superiority of one religion above all others led to suicide bombers willing to kill thousands of innocent civilians believed to be infidels. While it would be inaccurate to assert that this was the sole reason for 9/11, religious exclusivism was a contributing factor. These actions were extreme, but in studying Christian history I find that my own faith tradition has been guilty of similarly senseless acts of murder. The Crusades and the Inquisition occurred. How can I say with conviction that something similar will never happen again? I cannot change what those in other faith traditions believe or do. I cannot change what those in my own faith tradition believe or do. But I can change what I believe and do. The assertion that Jesus is the only way to God does not seem harmful on the surface, but it is this belief that has led to the deaths of innocent men, women, and children. Religious exclusivism has led to unfettered violence throughout the centuries; the historical record is clear. It is equally clear to me that I must follow a path for evangelism that is hospitable to the truth claims of other traditions.

Fireweed Evangelism, whether engaged in for personal or global reasons, is that path for me. To what path might God be leading you?

Chapter 4

Finding Your Own Path

As you begin seeking your own path, perhaps my method of discovery can be of help. Like mine, your path for evangelism will most likely be related to your autobiography. I now realize that before beginning my journey I had to confront my own baggage related to evangelism, the evangelism elephant that resided deep within my soul and psyche. My particular evangelism elephant was the "born again," "you must be saved by Jesus" approach. Your elephant may be something completely different, such as fear of talking about your faith, fear of not knowing enough about Christianity, or fear of being perceived as pushy or intrusive.

Most Christians have had some experience related to evangelism, even if only of answering a knock on the door to find Jehovah's Witnesses on the other side. The evangelism experiences that have had the greatest impact on me were during college with the Campus Crusade for Christ movement, which I have discussed, and as a child in the 1950s at a Southern Baptist church with my grandparents. I can remember, as if it were yesterday, sitting in the pew listening to the preacher expound in a loud voice on the physical attributes of hell. I remember most vividly his description of it as a place where "worms eat your eyeballs." Yes, that is what he said, and it put the fear of God in me, to put it mildly. Such scare tactics led me to believe for many years that religion was simply a list of things you did not do in order not to end up in hell. I went to church, to be sure, but I was not spiritual; I was not nurtured by my faith. As a result, I never considered answering the "altar call" that often followed such preaching; there was nothing about that approach that attracted me to the Christian faith.

Miraculously, God gave me the opportunity to confront this evangelism elephant almost forty years after I had first encountered it. The person God sent to help me do so was the evangelism leader of our clergy conference, who lived and ministered within thirty minutes of the town in Tennessee where I had first heard the preacher's harrowing description of hell. This time, however, I had traveled many more miles on my journey, and I was seminary educated and ordained. As a result, I had the tools to analyze why that particular method of evangelism was not right for me.

When I confronted the elephant within myself, the elephant was suddenly gone — kaboom — just as if it had been in a grand magic show. One minute it was there as big as life; the next it was gone without a trace. Then, and only then, the pathway opened up and the light shone through. I still did not know which way to go, but I knew, perhaps for the first time, that there were other ways, other paths to follow.

What a gift God gave to me; what a gift God has just waiting for you! They are there for the taking if only we know where to find them. Let me help you begin to discover yours.

Exercise 1 — Encountering Your Elephant
(If you have never had a negative experience of evangelism, proceed to Exercise 2)

Take some time in one of the following settings to reflect upon your own most significant memories of evangelism. You can be (1) alone in meditation, (2) alone while journaling, (3) with a trusted friend or clergy, or (4) in a small group. You might play meditative music to set the mood or light a candle. This exercise works well if someone can lead you through the meditation, but you can also do this alone if that works better for you. Give yourself at least forty-five minutes of uninterrupted time and pause for several moments after each sentence.

Slowly breathe in and out. Get a visual image of yourself as you begin your journey. How old are you? What are you wearing? How do you feel?

Stand at the threshold of your path. What state or country are you in? What does your path look like? Does it go up a hill, through the woods, by a beach? Where is it? Is it a bright sunny day or is it toward dusk or at night? Imagine yourself beginning to walk along it. As you're walking, think about the word "evangelism." What memories come to mind? What is your reaction to those memories? Is anyone else with you? Who? Picture them.

What are your feelings? Allow yourself to feel them; write them down if that's helpful. What would you like to say to the person or persons who presented you with your first experiences of evangelism? Slowly breathing in and out, form those words in your mind. Say them, either silently or aloud. Tell these people good-bye and continue walking down your path.

Let your negative memories of evangelism come to the surface. Picture them as a large elephant blocking your path. What does your elephant look like? Is it a cute, baby elephant or a large menacing one? Is it scampering about or standing still? Pray for all the people connected with your evangelism elephant. Offer up to God all your feelings connected with this experience. Put these feelings in God's hands. What would it take to move beyond your evangelism elephant? Can others help you? How about Jesus? Who comes to your aid? Picture these people. Talk to them. Would you prefer to walk around the elephant and wave good-bye? Would you rather physically move it off your path? Would you like to keep it there? The decision is yours. Imagine yourself interacting with your elephant and if you prefer, moving beyond it in whatever way is best for you.

Sit in silence for as long as necessary, and then gradually come back to the present moment. If you are alone, spend some time in reflection or in journaling. If you are with someone else or in a group, you may want to share your experience with those around you. Let your new reality sink in for at least a week before beginning Exercise 2.

Exercise 2 — Discovering Your Motivation

If you participated in Exercise 1, you may have found that you had an evangelism elephant blocking your path. Perhaps it was large and menacing and you felt better just scurrying around it as quickly as possible or maybe you had to forcefully push it out of the way. If you did not participate in the first exercise, then you probably do not have any negative associations with evangelism. Whatever is true for you, you should have a clear path ahead of you now.

There is an old Quaker proverb, "Proceed as the Way Opens." So — let's proceed! To discover the method of evangelism that is right for you will require some thinking and praying about your spiritual journey. Again, allow forty-five minutes of uninterrupted time. You may, as in Exercise 1, be alone or with others. You may wish to play meditative music or light a candle. Pause for several moments after each sentence.

Breathe slowly in and out several times. Begin thinking about why you go to church. Why do you get up on Sunday mornings instead of sleeping in, staying home to read the Sunday paper, spending time with friends, getting caught up on household chores, going to a second job, taking children to soccer games? As the popular saying goes, "What's in it for you?" How would your life be different if you did not attend church?

Now imagine yourself at a worship service. What is your favorite part of the service? The hymns, the sermon, the liturgy, the fellowship? Imagine that part of the service. What do you see, smell? What do you hear with the ear of the heart? What do you feel? Who is around you? As you leave the church, who is there? Who do you talk to? Imagine the conversation.

Picture yourself at a personal prayer time, some time in the past. Where are you? Is someone with you or are you alone? What are you praying for? How do you feel? Does this prayer experience in any way relate to why you come to church? If so, how? If not, do any of your other prayer experiences have a connection? If so, what is it? Could this piece of your autobiography provide a clue to your motivation for coming to church? Think about your different possibilities. As you think about your motivation for coming to church, could this same motivation provide you with a path for evangelism?

Keep walking down your path. What does it look like now? Are you alone or are others walking with you? Keep picturing yourself on the path. As your journey continues, you see a plant struggling to survive. It looks like it needs water, nurturance, and care. You see a babbling brook ahead of you with an old tin cup beside it. Fill the cup with water and water the plant. Do this as many times as it takes to water it adequately. You're getting tired now, so after you have finished you stop to rest. When you wake up the plant is revived — alive again!

You continue walking down your path. There are different paths for evangelism. I have said what mine turned out to be. Does God call you to this path or to another? Begin to get a sense of what your path might be through reflecting on your own life history, turning points, times of woundedness, and sources of healing.

My proximity to New York City made September 11 an integral part of my life story and therefore an integral part of my spiritual journey. Perhaps another national or world event has had a similar impact on you. What is it? Has it affected your view of Christianity? Does it relate in any way to your path for evangelism? How has your exposure to other religions, including Judaism, Islam, or the religions of other friends, affected your attitude to evangelism? Ask God to show you your specific path. Continue to breathe slowly in and out. Gradually come back to the present moment.

In participating in these exercises and addressing these questions, along with those asked earlier, hopefully you will discover your own reasons for being part of a Christian community. Out of that can come your motivation for inviting others to experience the same joy, sense of belonging, and peace that you have felt. What better reason could there be for engaging in evangelism — evangelism tailor-made for you!

Part II

CONTEXT

Repentance and forgiveness of sins
is to be proclaimed in his name to all nations.

– Luke 24:47 –

Chapter 5

Backyard Evangelism

I hope my journey has helped inform yours and that somewhere along the way you have become excited about reaching out and bringing others into the body of Christ. Once you have discovered your motivation and are ready to begin, one question needs to be addressed. To whom do you reach out?

We often think of evangelism as being carried out primarily in foreign lands. Europeans came to America to Christianize the indigenous Indian population. As America became established, numerous missionaries were sent to other countries, particularly developing nations, to bring the gospel to those who had never heard it. At the heart of this evangelistic or missionary work was a belief not only in the superiority of Christianity to all other religions, but also the belief that those who had not accepted Christ as their Savior would not be with God when they died. When this type of work was being undertaken, and heavily supported by most mainline denominations, America was predominantly a Christian nation. Now, those days are over. They no longer exist. We, as Christians, have no choice but to face that fact.

Statistics indicate that roughly 50 percent of the people in your community and mine choose not to attend church.[1] Traditional church growth literature refers to this population as the "unchurched." I have found, however, that this term itself can be offputting to those very people we seek to reach. Many of the "unchurched" consider themselves to be spiritual people who choose not to be involved in the institutional church. Some may have left the church for reasons they feel are quite valid. Others may be members of non-Christian faith communities. Viewing everyone who does not attend the institutional church as "unchurched" and therefore a potential "target" of evangelistic efforts can uphold a kind of Christian arrogance that has no place in our pluralistic culture. For this reason, I choose not to use this familiar terminology. My own evangelistic outreach would be to those who have left the church or who have no faith tradition. It would not be to Jews, Muslims, Hindus, Buddhists, or members of other religious traditions. Dialogue yes — evangelism no. This would, of course, affect the numbers of people available to evangelize, rendering it far less in some communities than the 50 percent figure.

In making this statement, I feel called to share with you an experience that gave me pause to reconsider my view. The first time I gave a workshop on this topic, an interesting mix of people were in attendance. As always, I began by inviting participants to share their own experience of evangelism. One of our most vocal participants was a woman, formerly of the Jewish faith, who had been introduced to Jesus by a friend; her life had never been the same again. Her countenance glowed with the love and peace of Christ in a way that was almost palpable.

During our first break I spoke with her and confessed immediately, "Your presence here blows one of my theories right out of the water!" She laughed because she had heard this before. She was very clear with me that she had spent much time in prayer and in conversation with her rabbi before making such a move. She was also clear that she was an exception to the rule. I share this story because it is real and true — very real for the woman involved, and true because it points out that there are no hard and fast rules in matters of the spirit. My conversation with this woman notwithstanding, I would still not evangelize a Jewish friend out of respect for the Jewish tradition. My evangelistic mission is to people with no present religious affiliation with whom I come in daily contact, people in my own backyard.

I vividly remember my church's missionaries in the 1950s, and they were certainly not in our backyard; they were in Laos. They were an attractive, young married couple. We had their pictures on a parish bulletin board; we sent them our church school nickels and dimes to help them tell other people about Jesus. We looked forward to regular letters from this faraway country. We were doing mission work. We were engaged in evangelism, and we knew the parameters and the manner in which to carry out that work.

But in America today, our mission as Christian people is primarily to our neighbors, co-workers, and relatives in our own country, our own communities. A simple recognition and awareness of this fact can change the way we perceive our relationships with those around us. It can also change the way we perceive ourselves. The following well-known poem rings true:

> Christ has no body now on earth but yours,
> No hands but yours, no feet but yours.
> Yours are the eyes through which Christ's compassion looks out
>   to the world;
> Yours are the feet with which he is to go about doing good;
> Yours are the hands with which he is to bless people now.[2]

Look in the mirror. You are the one Jesus has to bring others to the knowledge and love of him. You're it! It is at this level of awareness and recognition that the practical realities of backyard evangelism begin to manifest themselves.

First, as you begin to reach out to others in your community it is important to be aware of the religious context in which you live. Evangelism in an area in which Southern Baptists are a primary denomination will take one form; evangelism within a heavily Roman Catholic culture will take another; evangelism where there are numerous new age spiritualities will take yet another. No one method is right for all instances and no one method is always wrong. It is an issue of both/and rather than either/or.

Second, it is important to identify the primary group of people your church wants to reach. The maxim "Aim at nothing and you're sure to hit it" is true regarding evangelism. What particular group of people do you feel called to attract to your church? Young adults? Women who have left the church? Men who have left? Young families? Singles? The elderly? The poor? Those in need of healing? Carefully considering the needs of your community and the identity of your particular church will maximize your evangelistic efforts as a congregation. Planning programs and services to meet the needs of this group and then advertising those programs will also make a significant difference in your results.

Congregations attracted to the idea of Fireweed Evangelism would reach out principally to all those in need of healing — the healing balm of a relationship with Jesus Christ. What programming might reach this group? Weekly healing services with Holy Eucharist, a bereavement group that meets weekly or monthly, adult forums on the healing power of the risen Christ, youth group events that reach out to hurting teens, pastoral visitors to hospitals and prisons. The possibilities are limitless and would be determined by the spiritual gifts and passions within your church community. Such offerings made available to the wider community would attract those with this particular need. They would also give members a specific reason to invite a hurting friend to one of these events.

How about other groups within your community? Ask members of your church what they think. I was recently asked to give a workshop at a women's spirituality conference on a book I helped edit, *Women's Uncommon Prayers*. The majority of women at the conference had left the institutional church over the issue of inclusive language, and they were vocal about it. Most of the workshop participants had migrated to various women's spirituality groups that were not part of organized religion. It saddened me greatly to listen to one woman after another share her sense that the institutional church had become irrelevant to her spiritual life. Here was a group of women, seeking spiritual guidance and nurture, who were unable to find it in the church.

In *The Dance of the Dissident Daughter*, Sue Monk Kidd encapsulates the feelings of many of the women I met that day. She writes, "I was in an institution that celebrated fatherhood and sonship. I was in an institution created by men and for men. By the time I got home [from church] I felt disbelief that I'd not seen all this before — that the church, my church, was not just a part of the male-dominant system I was waking to, but a prime legitimizer of it."[3]

As I listen to our twenty-four-year-old daughter, Charlotte, talk about the church, I realize how antiquated it can seem to her age group. Inclusive language is a given for their generation, yet the church seems almost stuck in a time warp. As the graying of the church becomes increasingly evident, it seems as if many denominations continue to make decisions that keep a younger, vibrant population outside the doors of the church. Churchgoers then seem mystified as to why younger people aren't there. If more mainline denominations would regularly use the inclusive language liturgies they have painstakingly developed, it might begin to bridge the gap for this particular group.

Likewise, a focus on youth or young adult ministry will have consequences for church services and programming. If you really want to attract this group, talk to your members in these age groups. One church near a college campus has a Friday night coffeehouse called "Holy Grounds" with music and informal spiritual chats. After hearing complaints from many younger church members that the organ music "sounded like a funeral," another church changed to a guitar and drum band for one service. Again, the opportunities are limitless, but they do require a willingness to "do church" in a different way.

Third, before intentionally reaching out to people, it is important to understand who they really are, what makes them tick, what customs and needs they bring with them. Professor George Hunter relates that this was a component of St. Patrick's highly successful mission to the Celtic people of Ireland in the fifth century. As a young man of sixteen, Patrick was captured by pirates and forced into slavery in Ireland, where he worked for a prosperous tribal chief and druid. While there, he learned firsthand the culture of the barbarians who held him captive. When he was later freed, amazingly, he went back to evangelize the very people who had held him captive and whom he knew so well. His knowledge aided him in a number of ways. For example, Patrick knew that the number three was very powerful within the Irish culture. Triads of all sorts held great significance; they imagined some of their gods and goddesses in groups of three; one god was even believed to have three faces. As a result, when the Celts asked Patrick about the Christian God, Patrick explained God in Trinitarian terms of Father, Son, and Holy Spirit. While this would be confusing in most cultures, within the Celtic culture it was readily understandable and led to an acceptance of the Christian faith by barbarians who were deemed unreachable.[4]

Understanding of local culture is also evident at the Basilica of St. Maria Maggiore, or the Church of Mary Major, in Rome. Although, ironically, it is now known as one of Rome's four patriarchal basilicas, Sixtus III built the church in 432–40 to honor the Virgin Mary as the Mother of God. The site chosen for the basilica is an example of evangelism reaching out to people where they are. In the time of Sixtus in the fifth century, Roman women still frequented a temple of the mother-goddess Juno Lucina, which stood on the same hill. Since the women were accustomed to worshiping a female deity on the hill, it was easy for them to switch to worshiping the Virgin Mary in the same location. Christian evangelists of that age knew not only the beliefs but also the customs of the people they sought to reach.

How might this work in our own age? To reach women who have left the church due to its patriarchal language and structure, inclusive language liturgies become a key component of evangelism. To reach young people who feel the church is irrelevant, a willingness to experiment with different kinds of music in the service is important. To reach men who do not attend church, find out what makes them tick, what might attract them to the church. One congregation undertook a fundraiser in which single women could bring their car to church on a given Saturday and have it "tuned up" or "repaired" by a group of caring people in the congregation, most of whom were men who had rarely attended church previously. This event gave people with this skill a feeling of belonging, of being needed. Pick any group that is underrepresented in your church and ask, "How can we best meet them where they are?" Then devise a program to help you do that.

In Fireweed Evangelism, it is key that the evangelist understand the dynamics of the paschal mystery of death and rebirth through Jesus Christ. The process of figuratively dying and rising again through the healing balm of Christ lies at the heart of Fireweed Evangelism. Thus, understanding one's own experience of woundedness and healing in that light is key. Knowing how best to communicate this message to a particular person or group will depend on understanding who they are. Therefore, listening to a person's individual story is the beginning point and then gently sharing how their story intersects with the story of the paschal dynamic, Christ's story, is the next step.

Fourth, it is important to consider how your evangelistic efforts can contribute not only to the growth of your church, but also to its overall health. Since growth alone can actually disrupt the cohesion and health of a congregation, it is important to give serious consideration to other factors as well. This reality was made painfully clear to me in my first church. I was reporting on various newcomer projects at a meeting of lay leaders when one member raised her hand and said, "Elizabeth, that's what you're doing for people who aren't members here yet. What are you doing for us?" Her words startled me and my natural reaction would have been to be defensive. However, after reflecting on the programs and energies that were going into them, from her perspective, her words made sense.

So before embarking on a program for outreach to people outside your church, make sure your congregation's "inreach" programs are in place and running smoothly. What are your lay pastoral care programs — for those in crisis, in the hospital, the homebound? Before working on new member classes, make sure your Christian education for current members is up to par. Continually stress those systems and programs for current members while at the same time reaching out to include others in them. Over the years I have found that frequent reminders of programs for current members are necessary. Without them, the very members who were enthusiastic about reaching out to others will become defensive about their turf and their own need for the pastor's limited time.

In addition, other factors can contribute to a congregation's overall health and stability in the midst of growth. In March 2001, the Hartford Institute for Religion Research at Hartford Seminary issued the results of a comprehensive study known as Faith Communities in the United States Today. It is the largest survey of congregations ever conducted in the United States. Forty-one different religious groups, both Christian and non-Christian, participated with 14,301 surveys utilized. The study found that "heritage, vision, and moral commitment are three sources of cohesion for congregations. . . . Across liberal and conservative, Protestant and Catholic, Christian and non-Christian lines, these three values, when located in favorable social conditions, help contribute to congregational stability, vitality, growth, and fiscal health."[5]

Rather than focusing on those values or programs that contribute only to congregational growth, I have chosen this more holistic model, since church growth alone can disrupt congregational cohesiveness. It is to these three areas of heritage, vision, and moral commitment that I now turn.

Chapter 6

Heritage

Every morning on the way to work I pass a small church on the corner with a large, changeable message sign in the front yard. One day I was amused to read, "Under same management for two thousand years." It is often said of my suburb of New York City that people change jobs as often as they change clothes, but unfortunately it is not usually of their own volition. Frequent management changes are a very real problem, creating a world with little stability and anxious people.

How best to reach these people with backyard or, in this case, literally, front yard evangelism? By sharing a part of our Christian heritage that speaks directly to their need. The maxim "Jesus Christ — the same yesterday, today, and tomorrow" is one that is much needed today. Yes, we have been under the same management for over two thousand years. Let's advertise that part of our heritage in the midst of our ever-changing world.

In addition, we can highlight our biblical, denominational, and cultural heritages. All are significant and can be communicated in effective evangelism to our neighbors, friends, and co-workers.

Biblical Heritage

"Stories have to be told or they die, and when they die, we can't remember who we are or why we're here," reflects August at a home worship service in the best-selling novel *Secret Life of Bees*.[1] Too many people in your community and mine have forgotten who they are and why they are here. Nothing is more valuable than reminding us of this by sharing stories that have a central meaning in our lives, and no book has more meaningful stories than the Bible.

In *Biblical Perspectives on Evangelism: Living in a Three-Storied Universe*, Walter Brueggemann writes of evangelists primarily as storytellers of the ancient, transformational story of the biblical drama, who thereby participate in the transformational drama of the biblical story itself. He writes, "Evangelism means inviting people into these stories as the definitional story of our life, and thereby authorizing people to give up, abandon, and renounce other stories that have shaped their lives in false and distorting ways."[2]

As one of the premier Old Testament scholars of our age, Brueggemann focuses on stories within the Hebrew Scriptures as foundational to our lives as Christian people. The three stories that form the basis of his book are "the promise to the ancestors, the liberation of slaves, and the gift of land to displaced peasants."[3] This same three-part structure lies at the heart of Fireweed Evangelism and the paschal mystery upon which it is based: God's promise to us given through the life of Jesus Christ; Jesus' liberation of us from all that holds us captive; God's ultimate gift to us in the resurrection of Christ from the dead.

At the heart of our engagement with this biblical drama lies our willingness to be vulnerable, for without it we will never understand that from which we need to be liberated. Many times in my ministry I have tried to help people live into the fullness of God's promise to them. More times than I care to remember, however, there has been a system of denial in place that precludes their liberation from that which holds them in bondage. Until we can recognize and name that from which we need to be free, and own it, we will never experience the liberation Jesus offers us. Until we can acknowledge that from which we need to be healed, healing cannot occur. Again, it is Jesus' vulnerability on the cross that can give us the courage to be vulnerable ourselves.

In addition to this central biblical drama that lies at the heart of the paschal mystery, decide which individual Bible stories you might want to share with friends, neighbors, or co-workers. What is your favorite Bible story? Why? Has your favorite story changed over the years? It is helpful to share these reflections in small group discussions to gather a sense of the various parts of the Bible that speak to your fellow parishioners.

My favorite Bible stories as a child were often those centering on great heroics — David slaying Goliath, Moses parting the Red Sea, Jesus walking on water. Today, I focus more on those quiet stories of the still, small voice of God or of Jesus' positive relationships with women. For example, while Jesus is dining in Bethany at the home of Simon the leper, a woman breaks into the room carrying an alabaster jar. She then anoints Jesus' head with a very costly ointment. As a result, she is scolded by several of the men at the dinner, to which Jesus replies, "Let her alone; why do you trouble her?" (Mark 14:6). Her anointing can be viewed as a prophetic recognition of Jesus as the Christ, since a Messiah would receive such an anointing. So significant is her action to Jesus that he wants her to be remembered wherever the gospel is proclaimed in all the world. What an affirmation of her gift! Again and again Jesus affirms the very personhood of women throughout his ministry, completely against the social custom of his day. How many women long to hear this often unspoken aspect of the Christian faith! What might happen if people in your church shared this and other similar stories with their friends?

Next, you might discuss with others your favorite passages from the Letters of St. Paul. Did he write anything that seemed to be speaking directly to you? At what time in your life was this the case? My favorite Pauline passage is from his letter to the Romans, "For I am convinced that neither death, nor life, nor angels, nor rulers, nor things present, nor things to come, nor powers, nor height, nor depth, nor anything else in all creation, will be able to separate us from the love of God in Christ Jesus our Lord" (Rom. 8:38–39). I have often turned to this passage during difficult times and been uplifted by these words, written so long ago. Many times I have shared them with others when they also needed to hear a word of comfort. This passage is very relevant and powerful in light of my call to engage in Fireweed Evangelism. Your favorite biblical stories and passages will most likely shed light on your call as well. If you share your favorite passages with others in a non-threatening way and your fellow parishioners do likewise, a diverse group of people will indeed find themselves attracted to your church.

In addition to sharing Bible stories, inviting seekers to engage the Christian story in a dynamic way is another avenue for sharing our heritage with those who seek answers to the deeper questions of life. Many rich resources have been successfully used to share our heritage. For example, a course called Alpha is a fifteen-session program that runs over a ten-week period, providing a practical introduction to the Christian faith for both seekers and churchgoers alike. With what some consider to be a more conservative theological focus, the course combines fellowship with learning. Each class begins with a family-style supper, followed by a worship song, videotaped presentation, and small group discussion about the Christian life. Questions addressed are "Who is Jesus?" "How and why do I pray?" "How does God guide us?" and "Does God heal today?" The Alpha leader functions as a host, hospitably welcoming the new person into the Christian community of faith.

Via Media, designed to help Episcopalians and people of all faith traditions, focuses on an inclusive gospel message. It is an eight-week curriculum presented in a format of meal, videotape, workbook, and small group discussion. Topics covered range from Scripture and the Holy Spirit to Sin and Hope. Unlike similar evangelistic video-based curricula, Via Media relies on the Anglican three-legged stool of Scripture, Tradition, and Reason, rather than Scripture alone as its authority. It is designed to reach seekers who are just starting to consider the church, as well as people who have been hurt by the church who are looking for a way to return to their faith in a place that welcomes them for who they are.

A third resource is Klara Tammany's *Living Water: Baptism as a Way of Life,* which contains an impassioned, holistic approach to adult Christian education. The book focuses on the Episcopal baptismal covenant phrase by phrase, containing eight sessions filled with poetry, prayers, and biblical resources along with reflection questions. It is intended for use by all Christians, including those who are just beginning their spiritual journeys. The program is easily adaptable to any denomination.[4]

Denominational Heritage

All mainline denominations have a rich heritage on which to draw. This is clearly one of the strengths we have to offer those who do not currently attend church. Yes, there is less denominational loyalty today and people tend to shop for a church, but let others know the richness of your particular tradition and be proud of it. A first step in relating our heritage to others is understanding it ourselves. Does your church have a strong adult education program? Good adult forums on the history of your denomination are important. A good video series can bring your history to life and most denominations have them available.

Before communicating about your heritage, spend some time thinking about which aspect of your denomination's tradition speaks to you most powerfully. Is it the focus on the spoken word, the sermon? The liturgy? The history of mission work? The history of social witness? The role of lay ministers? Decide what attracts you, and then research where that fits into the Christian story, as well as the story of your particular denomination.

In addition, every judicatory (diocese, synod, conference, association, convention) has a heritage of missionary work within it. Without such work, your congregation would not exist. At the 218th Convention of the Episcopal Diocese of New Jersey, Assisting Bishop David Joslin unveiled an icon of the two primary missionaries to the diocese, John Talbot and George Keith. Most people in attendance had never heard of them until that moment. There is power in their images and in the story of their lives that can be transformative for missionaries in those same communities today. This icon stays on the fireplace mantle in our Diocesan House, serving as a constant reminder and inspiration to those who reach out to others in the same part of God's kingdom today. Who were the first missionaries for your denomination in your region? What obstacles did they overcome? How did they overcome them? Learning what worked in the past can provide clues as to how to proceed today.

Cultural Heritage

Congregations with the strongest sense of heritage are those in which ethnic populations dominate. Sixty-four percent of the predominantly Latino congregations and 50 percent of the predominantly black congregations ranked their sense of heritage as very high. In fact, such churches within the U.S. religious community are often used as a means of preserving racial/ethnic heritage. If the focus on ethnicity is carried too far, it can be a barrier to attracting diverse members; however, when kept in balance it is positive.[5]

Communicating our diverse cultural heritage is important to evangelistic success, but first we must in fact *be* culturally diverse. How can we best become a more culturally diverse worshiping community? Through intentional, well-structured evangelism to minority populations. While there are numerous ethnic minorities in the United States today, I would like to focus on the largest two — the African American community and the Hispanic community. Following the precepts of sound, creative evangelism, to successfully work in these communities we must first take the time to understand who they are — their culture, their needs, their religious heritage.

I will never forget my first day of involvement in outreach ministry to an African American community in Trenton, New Jersey. At the time, I was a lay minister in nearby Princeton, a radically different community from the one in which I felt God was calling me to serve. The Rev. Brian McCormick, the Catholic priest who had instituted Martin House thirty years before, took one look at me when I arrived and bluntly asked, "What do you think you're doing here? I'm not sure I want to subject my people to a white do-gooder from the 'burbs!" Needless to say, this was not the response I had expected. He then went on to add, "Don't expect me to thank you for working here. You should thank me for giving you a place to work out your salvation." Not one to be silent in the face of confrontation, I replied, "Has it ever occurred to you that the Holy Spirit may have called me here, just like the Holy Spirit called you? The ordained have not cornered the market on the Holy Spirit, you know."

Well, I guess he decided that I could stand up for myself enough to last more than a day or two in his environment, and I was on board. In fact, I had no idea if the Holy Spirit had called me there or if I was there out of some sense of privileged guilt. It was only five years later, when still working in the community, that I could say, "Yes, I believe the Holy Spirit may have had something to do with this."

One of my greatest learnings from my time at Martin House is that while I knew basically nothing about the African American culture and value system beyond stereotype, the people with whom I ministered knew a great deal about white values and white culture. How could they not? They were surrounded with it daily through television, advertisements, books, and at school. White middle-class values were held up as the way to succeed in life. As a result, my first two years of teaching in this community were spent thinking that I knew who my students were, what mattered to them, what their dreams were. They knew well what I wanted to hear from them, and hear it I did. Only when I had been among them for several years did they begin to let me into their lives in a way that made me realize that, in fact, I had not known my students at all. Evangelism within ethnic communities must first begin with a posture of listening — listening to the needs of the communities we seek to evangelize, listening to a sense of their identity as members of an ethnic group. Only then can we even begin to get a sense of how we as a church might best respond to them as individuals and as a community.

In *Evangelism in the African American Community*, Louis R. Jones articulates the unwritten rules that tend to keep African Americans from joining mainline denominations today:

1. Act like us.

2. Believe what we believe.

3. Worship like us.

4. Be good people.

5. Eventually, become exactly like us.

In reflecting on decreased attendance in all mainline denominations, including the predominantly African American churches within those denominations, he writes, "The church of yesterday that got us to this point is not the same church of tomorrow that will move us forward."[6]

What might the church of tomorrow look like? One answer for Jones lies in offering blended services, where tradition is honored yet freedom of expression is allowed. Drawing on Robert Webber's *Planning Blended Worship* he writes, "Blended worship is characterized by three concerns: 'to be rooted in the biblical and early church traditions, to draw from the resources of the entire church, and a radical commitment to contemporary relevance.'" In addition, Jones makes clear the centrality of preaching to the African American worship experience. "It is a certainty that an African American church will die without inspirational preaching."[7] The same could be said of those multiethnic churches that wish to keep African American members.

Jones then goes on to outline specific needs in the African American community that cry out to be addressed by any church that would seek to serve this population: the social and economic crisis within the African American family, reaching the African American male, and breaking the chains of drug abuse. Reading Jones's book, or others like it, and then listening with an educated ear to those within the African American community is a good beginning point for those who seek to evangelize in that community today.

Manuel Ortiz strikes a similar chord in *The Hispanic Challenge: Opportunities Confronting the Church*, while making it clear that evangelism in the Hispanic community is complex given the language differences and the fact that there is a wide discrepancy between first- and second-generation Hispanics in terms of religious expression. In addition, addressing the question of identity is complex. "The Federal Interagency Committee on Education defined Hispanic in 1975 as 'a person of Mexican, Puerto Rican, Cuban, Central American, or South American, or other Spanish culture or origin, regardless of race.'" Thus, Hispanic people are from a variety of cultures and races; as a result evangelistic efforts must be modified to each. Efforts to reach out to Hispanics are critical to the growth of the church today. Hispanics are the fastest growing minority population in the United States, experiencing a 61 percent rate of growth from 1970 to 1980 and a 53 percent rate of growth from 1980 to 1990. By the year 2000 there were 32.8 million Hispanics in the United States; by 2002 there were 37.4 million. In that same year one of every 7.5 Americans was Hispanic.[8]

The significance of this data to the church cannot be overstated. To remain viable, mainline Protestant denominations need to reach out to the Hispanic populations in their communities, but how to begin? Again, the answer lies in beginning from a posture of listening — listening to the stories of our Hispanic neighbors who are first-generation

Americans, as well as to their children and grandchildren who are second- or third-generation.

Manuel Ortiz, whose parents came to New York City from Puerto Rico in 1936, relates this part of his story:

> My friends and I ... felt torn between two worlds: the one we experienced at home and the one we faced on the streets.... No one at home spoke English and no one my age spoke Spanish on the streets.... As time went on, values and language aspects of my culture were being stretched into a new reality.... Though I lived in a mixed neighborhood comprised of Hispanics, African-Americans, and Italians, other areas were culturally defined. I was chased or robbed at times by Italians because I was Puerto Rican. I was a stranger in the African-American community because I was Puerto Rican. I had to make survival my top agenda every day. As I grew older, I began to wonder about my identity.

Where does the church fit into Ortiz's life and the life of those like him? He states clearly that the majority of first-generation Hispanics, like his parents, are Roman Catholic and that the Catholic Church concerns itself primarily with meeting the needs of those who retain the values of their country of origin, thus, not meeting the needs of the younger, second- and third-generation Hispanics. Ortiz sees this latter group as ripe for evangelism by mainline denominations today. Like Jones, Ortiz finds one answer to reaching his community in the structure of the worship service itself: through two separate services, one in Spanish and one in English; through one bilingual service; or through house churches known as growth cells.[9]

It is also important to get a sense of whether the Hispanic population in your community is Mexican American, Cuban American, Central American, and so on. In listening to their stories, you might ask them to relate what they perceive of as the differences between the various Hispanic communities. A lack of understanding in this area can lead to disastrous consequences. For example, in one Episcopal diocese there were two Hispanic churches in an inner-city area, only several miles apart. When one congregation began to dwindle in size and their priest moved to another parish, the diocese tried in vain for five years to merge the two congregations. Only after much futile effort and many lost members did the diocesan hierarchy realize the impossibility of blending a predominantly

Cuban congregation with a predominantly Mexican congregation. Church members must educate themselves about the realities of Hispanic ministry, not only to evangelize Hispanics who are outside the church, but also to keep those who are already within it.

If your church is predominantly Caucasian in makeup and there are significant minority populations in your area, an intentional focus on becoming a multiethnic church can bear much fruit. The institutional church could be a model for cooperation among those of different race and ethnicity, yet instead Sunday morning is the most segregated time of the American week. Given our common unity in Jesus Christ, we have a natural basis for fellowship and ministry together that too often goes unrealized. For an excellent "how-to" manual on becoming a multiethnic church, see Manuel Ortiz, *One New People: Models for Developing a Multiethnic Church.*[10]

A focus on our biblical, denominational, and cultural heritage will not only attract people to our congregations, it will help our churches maintain the cohesiveness and stability needed during a period of growth. Since growth alone can destabilize a congregation, a simultaneous focus on heritage can provide the needed glue to keep older members involved as newer members join your faith community.

Chapter 7

Vision

Our family recently attended sailing school, ready for whatever unknown adventure lay ahead. We began on small boats and eventually worked our way up to larger, seaworthy vessels. To our surprise, what we learned had as much to do with teamwork, communication, and vision as it did with sailing. The first time I sailed on my own, I learned how difficult it can be to get where you want to go. When I was ready to head into shore, I thought my vision was very clear — get to shore. I thought I was headed in the right direction, but suddenly the boat stopped and would not move an inch, even though there was wind all around me. So I started to work at making the boat move forward. I shifted my weight, tried to propel the boat with the rudder, and prayed. However, I soon learned that to catch the wind, I sometimes had to move my boat in a completely different direction. At other times, my boat was headed in the right direction, but I had to trim my sails to pick up the wind. With those adjustments, the boat sailed swiftly to shore with little effort on my part.

So it is with the church. We can think we have discerned the right vision for our particular congregation. We can put tremendous effort into implementing our vision, but sometimes we simply do not move. The church does not grow, or perhaps declines; lay leaders burn out; clergy tear their hair out. God's spirit is blowing all around us, but we can't seem to catch it. The harder we work, the less we move, frustration abounds, and survival becomes the byword. What to do? We may need to turn our boat in a completely different direction or we may just need to trim our sails, but some adjustment is needed to put ourselves more in line with God's spirit and God's vision for us. When we are out of line with God's will for our church, we can expend tremendous amounts of time and energy with little to show for it. For this reason, nothing is more important to the health and forward movement of a congregation than having a prayerfully, carefully discerned vision or sense of purpose. The Dudley and Roozen study, *Faith Communities Today*, affirms this understanding: "Congregations with a clear sense of purpose feel vital and alive. In contrast to feelings of unity based on heritage (the past), this center of cohesion looks to the future.... Larger, newer and growing congregations most clearly report feelings of being vital and alive."[1]

To begin to gain an understanding of God's vision for your church, you might begin by asking these questions: What is our identity? To what mission does God call us in our community? How will we achieve it? To begin to address these questions, it is important to look at two clear mission imperatives in Scripture that lie at the heart of the Christian vision — the Great Commandment and the Great Commission.

The Great Commandment

The background for the Great Commandment occurs in the Gospel of Luke. Immediately after Jesus is tempted in the wilderness for forty days, he reads from the scroll of the prophet Isaiah: "The Spirit of the Lord is upon me, because he has anointed me to bring good news to the poor. He has sent me to proclaim release to the captives and recovery of sight to the blind, to let the oppressed go free, to proclaim the year of the Lord's favor" (Luke 4:18–19). In effect, this is Jesus' mission statement articulated at the beginning of his earthly ministry, and it is clearly linked to the Great Commandment.

In the Great Commandment Jesus tells us, "'You shall love the Lord your God with all your heart, and with all your soul, and with all your mind.' This is the greatest and first commandment. And a second is like it: 'You shall love your neighbor as yourself.' On these two commandments hang all the law and the prophets" (Matt. 22:37–40). Who is our neighbor? The poor, the captive, the blind, and the oppressed. Who among us at some time in our lives is not captive to something, blind to the needs of those around us, or oppressed by forces beyond our control? Who is our neighbor? Everyone. Even so, Jesus is clear that our neighbors are particularly those who are poor.

Significantly, congregations with strong outreach ministries to the poor are more likely to grow than those that do not minister to this population. The Dudley and Roozen study reveals: "Contrary to some published experts, congregations with a strong commitment to social justice and with direct participation in community outreach ministries are more likely to be growing than other congregations."[2] Historically, such involvement has not been associated with church growth. However, it clearly seems to be the case in this comprehensive, contemporary study.

This data is also consistent with research involving volunteerism in the United States. Since the 1950s secular volunteerism in the United States has increased 56 percent, but volunteerism in the church has *decreased* 18 percent.[3] These statistics explode commonly held assumptions that volunteerism in the church has declined due to two-career families, the rise in single-parent families, or the overscheduled lives of people in our society. Why aren't more people volunteering for the church?

Today, many secular volunteer efforts involve hands-on ministry to the economically disadvantaged: Habitat for Humanity, inner-city tutoring programs, and work with the homeless, to name a few. When the church provides hands-on opportunities primarily for committee work or those activities that maintain the church, it can lose out on the passion many people have for freely giving their time to significantly help the poor in their communities. In addition, the church can provide something that secular agencies cannot — conversation about these efforts in light of the teachings of Jesus Christ. Such reflection, based on these sermons in action, enables the church to lead people into a deeper understanding of the gospel message.

While there are many ways to respond to the Great Commandment, I would like to focus on one — outreach to the poor. Churches with this call might begin with education on the biblical basis for doing so. Questions that can be addressed are: What are the biblical reasons for such ministry? How do we as Christian people relate to the poor as we offer them community in the body of Christ? Who are the poor?

Throughout the history of Christianity, some scholars have interpreted "the poor" to mean the poor in spirit. Yet such interpretation is not in line with the meaning of the New Testament Greek word for "poor," *ptochos,* which means "one who does not have what is necessary to subsist and is forced into the degrading activity of begging." In A *Theology of Liberation*, Gustavo Gutiérrez speaks out against all attempts to transform poverty into spiritual poverty. He writes of "the brute reality of material poverty, [as] lack of sufficient economic goods to lead a full human life, which describes perhaps 70 percent of the human family."[4]

Part of this 70 percent of the human family lives somewhere in your community and mine. Regardless of how affluent a community is, there are nearly always those living below the poverty line nearby. It is important to minister to people in developing nations, but if we ignore those in our own backyards, we are missing something.

Before I began to minister at Martin House in Trenton, I was reminded of the poor primarily in Sunday morning sermons or weeknight news reports. On such occasions, my mind was filled with images of people of color in inner-city settings, of the rural poor throughout our own country, and of masses of hungry, poverty-stricken people in developing nations. My feelings of compassion and concern for these nameless people were often overshadowed by a sense of my own inability to change anything, leaving me with a sense of frustration and helplessness. But since I was able to extend hospitality to the poor through my work at Martin House, they are no longer an abstraction. The poor are Myrtle, Lamar, Emma, Anna, Scott, and Resa. I know now that the poor are parents who have hopes and dreams that their children will have a better life. They are women and men with specific goals for their own lives, who need help in overcoming the many obstacles encountered in reaching them. The poor are people who share our human condition — the joy, as well as the pain, the relief, as well as the suffering.

Kierkegaard wrote, "Religiousness is suffering, not for its own sake, but suffering through participation in the suffering of the world and the world's anguish." God has offered all of us many different ways in which to participate in the pain and suffering of our neighbors, joining their stories with our own, if only for a moment. But first we must not only see the needs around us, but act on the needs we see. "If a brother or sister is naked and lacks daily food, and one of you says to them, 'Go in peace; keep warm and eat your fill,' and yet you do not supply their bodily needs, what is the good of that? So faith by itself, if it has no works, is dead" (James 2:15–17).

Both the Hebrew Scriptures and the New Testament are filled with further injunctions to help the poor. "If there is among you anyone in need, a member of your community in any of your towns within the land that the LORD your God is giving you, do not be hard-hearted or tight-fisted toward your needy neighbor. . . . Open your hand to the poor and needy neighbor in your land" (Deut. 15:7, 11). The prophet Jeremiah tells us that this is the way to know God. "He judged the cause of the poor and needy; then it was well. Is not this to know me? says the LORD" (Jer. 22:16). Scripture states that the Lord "says," not "asks." In *Unexpected News: Reading the Bible with Third World Eyes* Robert McAfee Brown writes: "The form of [this] construction allows only for an affirmative answer. Conclusion: to know God is to do justice and righteousness, to vindicate the poor and the needy."[5] In the Jeremiah passage, the Hebrew word for "poor" is *ani*, which means a person who occupies a lowly position and is dependent on those who are higher. The Hebrew word for "needy" is *ebyon*, which means one who is asking from others as a beggar. Here, as in the New Testament, the words do not refer to spiritual poverty.

Reaching out to the poor and the outcast was a hallmark of Jesus' ministry. He reasserts his claim to "bring good news to the poor" (Luke 4:18), when John the Baptist sends his disciples to ask Jesus if he is "the one to come." Jesus replies, "Go and tell John what you have seen and heard: the blind receive their sight, the lame walk, the lepers are cleansed, the deaf hear, the dead are raised, the poor have good news brought to them" (Luke 7:22). Moreover, his most famous teaching of all, the Sermon on the Mount, begins with concern for the poor: "Blessed are you who are poor, for yours is the kingdom of God. Blessed are you who are hungry now, for you will be filled" (Luke 6:20–21).

A poignant example of this blessedness is found in *The City of Joy* by Dominique Lapierre. In Calcutta, India, where three hundred thousand people are stranded on the streets and countless others live in one of three thousand slum areas, one would think hospitality would be a gift few could afford to give. Yet quite the opposite is true.

In these slums people actually put love and mutual support into practice. They knew how to be tolerant of all creeds and castes, how to give respect to a stranger, how to show charity toward beggars, cripples, lepers, and even the insane. Here the weak were helped, not trampled upon. Orphans were instantly adopted by their neighbors and old people were cared for and revered by their children.[6]

This same hospitality was revealed to me while I was leading Bible study at Martin House. We had just read Matthew 25, in which Jesus tells the righteous, "I was hungry and you gave me food, I was thirsty and you gave me something to drink" (Matt. 25:35). "How simple this gospel message is," I remarked, "yet how hard it is to live it in our daily lives." One of the participants, a woman of color from the impoverished community around us, replied, "I don't think it's difficult at all. When someone knocks on your door and they're hungry, you give them food. If they don't have a place to sleep, you let them sleep on your floor." I suddenly thought of the appeals for the Hunger Fund in my own church, and I realized how far removed I was from those who need my help. The poor do not knock on my door; they are comfortably at arm's length. Sitting face-to-face with this woman, who barely had enough to eat herself, brought me face-to-face with the reality of my protected life.

Not only are those of us who live in suburban communities often isolated from the poor in our middle-class neighborhoods, but church programs for the poor can perpetuate this distance. This type of "arm's-length ministry" with the poor is described in *Urban Perspectives*, a newsletter by Bob Lupton, a psychologist and lay evangelist in inner-city Atlanta:

> Our hearts compel us to care. And so we establish clothes closets and food pantries and benevolence budgets. But these do little more than ensure our protection from entanglement with the poor. . . . We create efficient systems rather than effective relationships. By our one-sided giving we retain control while remaining at arm's length from the recipients. It is an attempt to cure without community. And it is not the gospel![7]

Jesus makes it clear that in reaching out to the needy, we are not meant to "cure without community." Rather, we are to invite them to table fellowship with us. "When you give a luncheon or a dinner, do not invite your friends or your brothers or your relatives or rich neighbors, in case they may invite you in return, and you would be repaid. But when you give a banquet, invite the poor, the crippled, the lame, and the blind. And you will be blessed, because they cannot repay you, for you will be repaid at the resurrection of the righteous" (Luke 14:12–14). Jesus' injunction is to offer community, in addition to food, clothing, and the basic necessities of life.

In discussing such hospitality, Barbara, a seasoned lay minister with the poor, expressed concern about the practicalities involved. "Our church has a food pantry and administers housing funds," she stated. "Many of those we serve often have serious drug or alcohol problems. Frankly, most of us are not equipped to deal with problems of this magnitude." It is important for churches that undertake ministry with poor people not to romanticize them. Indeed, some of them have problems with alcohol, drugs, or other dependencies, just as do some members of the host church. Ways of dealing with these and other realities should be discussed prior to undertaking this ministry.

To offer "community with a cure," Grace Church in Plainfield, New Jersey, established an after-school choir program for children ages six through twelve. Applicants were chosen on the basis of financial need. Most participants were from homes of the working poor, who were unable to afford standard after-school programs. Students were picked up after school in a Red Cross van and brought to the church, where they enjoyed one-on-one tutoring and recreation, in addition to the choir instruction.

To establish such programs that enable effective relationships to occur, rather than merely an efficient system to be in place, requires careful, prayerful preparation by a congregation. First, churchwide adult education can be offered to introduce the concept of "Fireweed Hospitality." Session 1 of the Hospitality Evangelism Workshop (page 123) is designed for this purpose. In preparing for the workshop, keep in mind that questions may be raised about offering hospitality that embodies a "cure with community." Both the challenges and promises of this ministry can be addressed.

At the close of the workshop, you might want to ask for volunteers who are interested in developing a program for reaching out to the poor in your community. From this group, a team can be formed to conduct a Community Needs Assessment. Since ownership of the program is critical, it is best for the assessment to be conducted by an interested group of laypeople, rather than by a seminarian or an outside consultant. The team members can interview directors of a variety of local agencies such as the YMCA, YWCA, Red Cross, Salvation Army, city or county welfare, local hospitals, food pantries, area churches, area schools, and other local social outreach agencies. An interview form for this purpose can be found on page 138.

Once the interviewers determine the kinds of needs that are not currently being met, they can begin to discuss which of those your church might be able to address. At this point, the team can consider these questions: What kinds of programs will enable effective relationships to develop? What are our talents and skills? Where are we willing to invest large amounts of our own time and energy? Most important, where is the Spirit leading us as we seek to serve God by making the connection between our faith and our works?

When these questions have been addressed, an outreach proposal can be written and distributed to the congregation, outlining several different possibilities for ministry with the poor that will enhance relationship building. Attached to the proposal can be questions for reflection and discussion, to be used at an adult education event or for a special retreat day for interested parishioners.

As your church embarks on this ministry, it is important to keep in mind that the purpose is not to serve the needy as clients, as "us" versus "them." Ministry is meant to be *with* the poor, not *to* the poor. This outreach ministry should not be entered into with a paternalistic attitude of superiority, implying that members of the host church have all the answers to give. Quite the opposite is true. In reaching out to the poor, we are not only reaching out to our sisters and brothers in Christ, but to the many gifts they bring with them for us. In a ministry of relationship, regard for other people's vulnerability and delight in their offerings to us presupposes that we perceive them as equals, as people who share our common humanity. Thomas Ogletree writes of this equality of host and stranger that results in reciprocal acts of hospitality, where both parties have much to give and to be given, thereby at times reversing the guest/host roles.[8]

As relationships develop, volunteers in the program can be encouraged
to invite participants to worship at the host church if they do not currently
attend church or are looking for a new church home. It is important that
we, as the body of Christ, welcome others into the body, that they may
know the life-giving experience of worship in a community of faith. It is
equally important, however, to keep in mind that certainly some of those
to whom we minister will be members of other faith traditions; therefore,
their choice of faith should be treated with dignity and respect, rather
than a desire to convert.

Lay ministers involved in hands-on outreach ministry will need training, support, and ongoing reflection. This ministry can raise numerous
questions that may need to be dealt with from a spiritual perspective by
a trained leader. A monthly co-workers' meeting, offering prayer, Bible
study, time for reflection, and sharing of experiences, is most helpful in
preventing volunteer burnout and in meeting the needs of those involved.
At each meeting, attending to one's own spiritual needs can be discussed
with co-workers. In Mother Teresa's clinic for lepers in Calcutta, India,
the following Hindu poem hangs on the wall:

> If you have two pieces of bread,
> Give one to the poor,
> Sell the other,
> And buy hyacinths
> To feed your soul.

This poem offers a much-needed reminder of the importance of self-care
to those who minister in the name of Christ.

As we develop programs to respond to the call of the Great Commandment by reaching out to our neighbors in need, it is important to keep one
thought at the center of our hearts. As Henri Nouwen writes in *Reaching
Out: The Three Movements of the Spiritual Life*, this ministry of hospitality,
like all others, "points to someone higher than our thoughts can reach,
someone deeper than our hearts can feel and wider than our arms can
embrace, someone under whose wings we can find refuge (Psalm 90) and
in whose love we can rest, someone we call our God."[9]

The Great Commission

The Great Commission in the Gospel of Matthew has provided a mission focus for the church since the first century. After his crucifixion and resurrection, Jesus appears to the disciples and offers this often-quoted mission imperative, "Go therefore and make disciples of all nations, baptizing them in the name of the Father and of the Son and of the Holy Spirit, and teaching them to obey everything that I have commanded you" (Matt. 28:19–20).

The key verb in the original Greek passage in Matthew is *matheteuo*, which is literally translated "make disciples." This verb occurs only four times in the New Testament — three times in Matthew and once in the book of Acts. In Matthew 13:52 it refers to a person who "becomes a disciple in the Kingdom of heaven." In Matthew 27:57 the reference is to Joseph of Arimathea, who asks Pilate for the body of Jesus and then buries him. "When it was evening, there came a rich man from Arimathea, named Joseph, who was also a disciple of Jesus" (Matt. 27:57). Thus, Matthew does not use the verb to refer to seekers or those on the cusp of belief, but to those who are deeply committed disciples. Of the use of the verb *matheteuo* in the Great Commission in Matthew 28:19–20, Eduard Schweizer writes, "Unquestionably 'make disciples' contains the main verb, to which everything that precedes and follows is subordinate."[10] Therefore, it is the key word in this command of Jesus.

The only way to "make disciples" is through conversion, a turning of the heart toward Jesus. Thus in this resurrection appearance, Jesus commissions his disciples to convert others to a belief in him as the resurrected One. Who are the others to which he refers? All nations or all peoples. For centuries, the Christian church has interpreted Jesus' words as a mandate to convert all people, all nations to Christianity, to make them disciples. Whereas the original statement in Matthew makes no reference to religious exclusivism, it has been misused to support an exclusivist claim of Christianity — Christianity is the one true religion; all others are false. However, a careful study of the context in which Jesus spoke these words reveals that exclusivity was not his intent. Jesus' original desire here is to make it clear that the Christian mission is to extend to the gentiles, not just to the House of Israel. That was one of the debates at the time this Gospel was written. The phrase "all nations" in Matthew 28:19 refers to universal discipleship, hearkening back to Matthew 10:18 which refers to the mission to the gentile nations.[11] Thus, it can be argued that the Great Commission in Matthew is meant to be inclusive in intent, rather than exclusive.

Additionally, in terms of the mission of the church today, it is significant that the commissioning in Matthew does not stand alone but in conjunction with Jesus' commissioning of the disciples in the other two synoptic Gospels, Mark and Luke, as well as in Peter's description of this commissioning in the book of Acts. *Only in Matthew are the disciples told to "make disciples" of all nations.* In Mark, Jesus says, "Go into all the world and proclaim the good news to the whole creation" (Mark 16:15). In the Gospel of Luke, Jesus states that "repentance and forgiveness of sins is to be proclaimed in his name to all nations" (Luke 24:47). In the book of Acts, Peter tells the Gentiles that in a post-resurrection appearance, "He [Jesus] commanded us to preach to the people and to testify that he is the one ordained by God as judge of the living and the dead" (Acts 10:42). The Greek verb used in Mark, Luke, and Acts is *keryxate,* which is translated "proclaim" or "preach." The verb is used fifty-nine times in the New Testament, almost fifteen times as often as the verb *matheteuo,* translated "make disciples." There is an important distinction between these three commissioning passages and the one in Matthew. Proclamation or preaching does not explicitly imply conversion; it can just as readily be used dialogically. It does not imply the type of evangelistic approach that views the Christian's role as that of converter, but rather implies that God will do the converting, if that is God's will.

Is it God's will that a modern-day Jew become a disciple of Christ, or that a Buddhist or Hindu become a disciple of Christ? We cannot know. Thus, the verb "proclaim" or "preach" feels more appropriate to me within the context of evangelism today than does the verb "make disciples." Titus Presler echoes this perspective in his book *Horizons of Mission.* He writes, "Living with other religions becomes a quandary for Christian mission only when mission is understood, as it so often is, simply as 'trying to convert other people.' The first fruit of Christian experience is neither a condemnation of other religions nor a conversion campaign but joyful and natural witness to the presence of the triune God in one's life."[12] Such joyful, natural witness is embodied in the word "proclamation." Thus, the distinction between the commissioning statement in Matthew, and the statements in Mark, Luke, and Acts are important to hold before us in our pluralistic world. Since two of the three synoptic Gospels focus on "proclamation" rather than "making disciples," as does the book of Acts, and proclamation is more in keeping with a dialogical view of evangelism, it is to this concept that I now turn.

Proclamation

How can we best proclaim the gospel in our own age? When proclamation is discussed, it is usually in terms of preaching by the ordained few. However, I would like to focus on four ways that all Christians, both lay and ordained, can proclaim the gospel: through faith, behavior, invitation, and communication.

First, if we do not put our faith in Jesus to bring about the desired response, our evangelistic efforts will bear no fruit. Proclamation will go unnoticed and unheeded. A story in the Gospel of Luke succinctly makes this point. While at a lake, Jesus notices that several of his disciples who are fishermen have returned to shore without catching any fish. He turns to one of them, Simon, and says, "Put out into the deep water and let down your nets for a catch" (Luke 5:4). Simon makes it clear to Jesus that they have been fishing all night without catching a single fish, but agrees to try once again. When he does so, he catches so many fish the nets nearly break from the weight.

When the disciples go about their task alone they catch nothing, but the situation changes dramatically when they put their trust in Jesus. Simon does not believe he will ever be able to catch fish, given his past failure, but when Jesus appears and asks that he try again, Simon replies, "If you say so, I will let down the nets" (Luke 5:5). His faith in Jesus gives him the courage to try again. This time, not only do the disciples catch fish, they fill all of their nets and two boats to overflowing. Jesus is then clear when he tells the disciples, "From now on you will be catching people" (Luke

5:10). If it is our intent to "catch people" and bring them into the church today, we must also begin with Jesus firmly at our side. Without faith in him, through steadfast prayer, we will lose our way and no amount of planning, inviting, or communicating will bring others into our faith communities.

The second most effective way to proclaim the gospel is by living it each and every day to the best of our ability. A joke sent to me via e-mail brings this reality into stark relief.

A man pulls up to a red light behind one other car. He notices that the driver of the car in front of him is shuffling through some papers and talking on her cell phone. The light turns green, but the woman doesn't notice the light change. The man begins pounding on his steering wheel and yelling at the woman to move, but she will not budge. The light turns yellow. The man begins to blow his car horn, then rolls down his window and begins cursing. Hearing the commotion the woman looks up, sees the yellow light, and speeds through the intersection, just as the light turns red.

At this point the man is beside himself. He rants some more. As he is screaming, he hears a tap on his window, and looks up into the barrel of a gun held by a very serious-looking policeman. The policeman tells him to turn off his car, get out, and keep both hands in sight. The man is quickly cuffed and hustled into the patrol car. He is driven to the police station where he is fingerprinted, photographed, booked, and placed in a cell.

After several hours, a policeman approaches the cell and lets him out. He is escorted back to the booking desk where the original officer is waiting with his personal effects. The policeman says, "I'm sorry for this mistake, but you see, I pulled up behind your car while you were blowing your horn and cursing a blue streak at the car in front of you. I noticed the 'Jesus Loves All of Us' license plate holder, and the 'Follow Me to Church' bumper sticker, and the chrome-plated Christian fish emblem on the trunk, so naturally I assumed you had stolen the car."

Hmmm . . . I wonder how many people have been confused about what it means to be a Christian given our behavior. When the primary news about Christians is that we are fighting with one another over this or that belief, who would want to become one of us? Within our communities, when those who do not attend church see us losing our temper over small matters, participating in questionable business deals, engaging in road rage, exhibiting intolerance, gossiping, drinking too much, or spending too much on ourselves — what are we communicating to them about being a Christian? Walking the walk, not just talking the talk, is one of the most important aspects of evangelism. St. Francis of Assisi put it succinctly, "Preach the gospel at all times. When necessary use words." Our actions and attitudes proclaim loudly for all to see what it means to be a Christian, louder than most of us care to imagine. What we say will have less effect in terms of evangelism than what we do. For this reason the most important proclamation of the Good News is how we live it ourselves, how we demonstrate it in our own lives. Our daily behavior is a critical element in bringing others to the church or driving them away.

A third way of proclaiming the gospel is by simple invitation, which lies at the heart of Fireweed Evangelism. Reaching out to a hurting friend begins with prayer and then moves to an invitation to come to church to meet the One who has been wounded as have we and has overcome it. Not only does inviting lie at the heart of Fireweed Evangelism, it is the most successful, proven method for bringing others into the church. Research has shown that three out of four people who previously did not attend church now do so due to the simple invitation of a friend or co-worker who cared enough to invite them into their faith community.[13] If 75 percent of the people find their way across our thresholds by invitation, then this aspect of evangelism ministry is significant.

Providing structured opportunities for members to invite others to church is key. A yearly Hospitality Sunday or Invite-a-Friend Sunday provides a concrete reason for parishioners to extend an invitation in the name of Christ. Since people are most likely to be seeking a church during the Christmas and Easter seasons, as well as around Mother's Day, members can also be encouraged to invite friends at that time. In addition, friends can be invited to educational events geared to the community at large, events for young people, and even church dances for different age groups.

When I was a teenager, many of our dances were held at Canterbury House, the parish house of the local Episcopal church. Often on Friday nights a band of would-be high school rock stars played and everyone would gather there. I was a Methodist at the time so my attendance had nothing to do with denominational affiliation. The parish priest would simply wander in and out at the beginning of the evening, and we all thought he was "hip" (the word in vogue at the time). Thinking back on it, he said very little, but the fact that he made this space available to us and made an appearance communicated that he understood what was important to us at that time in our lives.

Communication is another key aspect of evangelistic outreach in our world today. It can include articles in the local newspaper; advertisements in Yellow Pages, newspapers, billboards, movie houses, and on local cable television stations; postcards mailed in a series; doorhangers; radio ministries and televised worship services on local cable channels. All communication efforts should include an attractive and professionally written web page. Judicatories or national church bodies might have a box at the top of their page that says, "Find a Church Near You." You click the box and then fill out your city, state, and zip code to find the church nearest you. One denomination's web page features a theme song that can be downloaded. The opportunities are as varied as our imaginations.

In addition, a superb model for reaching out to those outside our church communities is outlined in *Reclaiming the Great Commission*, written by Bishop Claude E. Payne of the Episcopal Diocese of Texas and Dr. Hamilton Beazley. Their comprehensive model outlines moving the church from maintenance to mission mind-set. Each congregation is viewed as a missionary outpost while the judicatory primarily serves as a resource for the congregation and supports the missionary vision. Their model is transformational, focusing on miraculous expectations of the gospel and living into them. Throughout their book, the authors make it clear that "evangelism is not a program of the Church; rather, it is the essential work of the Church."[14]

Whether your church focuses on the Great Commandment or the Great Commission or a combination of both, keep in mind that mission statements are important, even though historically they have been both overrated and underused. If your church develops a mission statement, make sure every member knows clearly what it is and can recite it "on the spot" when asked. For this to occur, mission statements need to be articulated at least once a month and in a number of different ways — in sermons, adult education events, bulletins, parish newsletters, etc. In addition, when asked, parishioners should be able to state several activities your congregation is involved in that are related directly to your mission.

Discernment

The field for mission work is ripe, with many opportunities awaiting us. What is the best way to discern which aspect of mission work your church might become involved in? The place to begin is with the laity, their passion and gifts for ministry. Regardless of the needs in your community and in your church, if the laity does not feel called to that particular ministry, a program designed to address that need will most likely not be successful.

Numerous programs have been developed to aid churches in this area. *Network: The Right People . . . In the Right Places . . . For the Right Reasons* is an outstanding one. It is not a skills inventory, but rather a comprehensive program to help people discover their unique blend of passion, spiritual gifts, and personal style. Network contains a Passion Assessment, helping participants answer the question, "Where should I serve?" When people serve in their area of passion, they are more motivated. Then spiritual gifts are discerned that answer the "what" question. What do I do when I serve? Next, a Personal Style Assessment is used to answer the "how" question? Am I structured or unstructured? People-oriented or task-oriented? When passion, gifts, and style are congruent, therein lies wholeness — not only for the individual but also for the church. *Network* can be used in a variety of formats, including eight forty-five-minute sessions, making it appropriate for Sunday morning adult education classes.[15]

In addition, my own Gift Discernment Retreat is included (pages 110–116). Retreats are an ancient Christian way to take time out from the fast pace of our lives, to slow down and reflect on God's will for us. Setting time apart leads to a different dynamic, one in which the structure of the time itself leads to necessary introspection and reflection. Just getting away from the many distractions of our lives can enable us to peel away the layers and look more clearly at our ourselves and our relationship with God. Then we are better able to answer the question, "What gifts has God given me and how am I to use them to help bring about the Kingdom of God here on earth?"

The necessary follow-up to this individual focus is a collective one. One of the simplest methods I have used with groups is also one of the most effective. It involves three questions:

1. If the Kingdom of God were to come in your community, what would it look like?

2. What is the current reality in your community, when compared with your vision of God's kingdom?

3. What will it take to get from here to there?

The answer to question three will tell you your mission.

In addition, visioning exercises with a vestry, session, board of trustees, or governing body are helpful in establishing an initial sense of mission. The elected leaders of a congregation can provide valuable insight into a possible mission focus. However, it is then necessary to take the exercise to the rest of the congregation. In doing so, be sure to include newcomers. Some of the best dreamers and visionaries are those with the least experience of the church.

The Visioning Workshop (pages 117–120) is designed to be used with a congregation or with a series of groups within a judicatory. Results can then be compiled and a vision leading to mission discerned. The first time I used this exercise with a congregation was during the time usually allotted for a sermon. The uniqueness of the approach was a welcome relief to many who had heard sermon after sermon in their years as church members. Meditative music played as the exercise was read. To my delight during the sharing time that followed, one fourth grader raised his hand and said, "I can play the trumpet. Maybe I can do that for the church." Then another boy raised his hand and said, "I can play drums." Then an older girl raised her hand, "I can play the flute." Suddenly, we had the beginnings of a band. So hold on! You never know what the Holy Spirit has in mind when you begin such an endeavor.

Churchwide discernment through a variety of means can lead to a vision for mission based on both individual and collective gifts. When your church is alive to the gospel in such an engaging way, others will naturally be attracted to it. Rather than leading to possible differences within the congregation between old and new members, this method of church growth leads to unity around a common vision.

Chapter 8

Moral Commitment

When my husband and I moved from Tennessee to New Jersey twenty-five years ago, I was in a state of culture shock for at least a year. Nowhere were regional disparities more evident than in the church's definition of what it meant to be a moral person. As a child and teenager in the 1950s and 1960s, I used to pray every night for God to help me be a good Christian person, i.e., a good moral person. To me and to others within my faith community that meant not breaking the Ten Commandments, along with the Eleventh unwritten but well-known commandment, "Thou Shalt Not Have Premarital Sex." Morality meant what I did in my private life; it meant being as pure as one could be personally. The only emanation outside of oneself was the other well-known mandate — the Golden Rule, "Do Unto Others As You Would Have Them Do Unto You." Again, however, this was interpreted as within the realm of one's personal relationships only. There was no sense of the wider body of Christ outside personal experience.

After we had lived in New Jersey for about five years, one Sunday morning the difference between my two experiences of church was brought home to me. Our church had hired a Visiting Theologian who happened to be from the South to teach and preach among us. That Sunday, he eloquently proclaimed that when the devil came, he would most likely be an attractive, charismatic individual wrapped in an American flag, singing "The Star-Spangled Banner." In other words, the devil would appear most unlike any vision we could have of evil incarnate. His words jolted me. "The devil? He's actually mentioning the devil?" I had not heard the devil referred to in any setting, much less in a sermon, since I had left the South. Why not? Did the devil not live in New Jersey?

In reflecting on this question, it began to dawn on me that while perhaps the devil was not discussed in my current parish, evil most definitely was, but it was almost always in terms of systemic evil — the evil inherent in unjust systems that oppress the poor and the marginalized. Interestingly, personal morality was seldom mentioned. Yet is it possible that God cares more about systemic evil than personal evil, or the other way around? Certainly this is an issue of both/and rather than either/or. It is significant that moral commitment serves not only as a source of cohesion in a church, but as a marker of those churches that are growing versus those that are declining in membership.

The moral commitment of a congregation can be summed up by how it lives out the Great Commandment to love one's neighbor as oneself. This is true in both the public and private spheres. Rather than being prescriptive about moral behavior, I find it most helpful to raise questions in light of a moral stance. Such questions can be addressed in a variety of settings — adult forums, cottage meetings, or the governing lay body of your congregation.

In terms of public morality, how committed is your church to actively loving the poor, the oppressed, the sick, the needy, the imprisoned within your community? What concrete outreach programs are in place to respond to these needs? Have you ever undertaken a needs assessment of your community? If not, why not? What percentage of your congregation is involved in hands-on ministry to these populations? Are efforts in place to bring others into this ministry? Could God be calling your church to begin a new ministry in this area?

Does your church take a public stand on issues related to your commitment, or does it shirk from such responsibility in fear of offending someone who might disagree? Is the church a moral beacon in the community to whom others turn for answers to difficult questions of public morality when they arise, or has the church "gone secular" and so blended in with its surrounding culture that it is basically indistinguishable from it?

What about personal decisions made in the workplace? Are business ethics regularly addressed in your church? We have only to look at the number of recent corporate scandals, e.g., Enron, WorldCom, and Tyco, to see the devastating impact of a lack of business ethics.

Is your judicatory committed in every situation to the rights of the victim, especially if the offender has been a member of the clergy? One has only to look at the recent situation in the Roman Catholic Church regarding sexual abuse by clergy to see the devastating impact when victim's rights are not upheld. Are clear guidelines and boundaries in place to protect the vulnerable on all levels?

In the realm of private morality, do adult forums and Sunday school classes focus on helping people live a personally moral life? Is there support for teens, parents, married persons, or those striving to live a moral single life? How seriously does your church take confession of sin? Has sin "gone out of vogue," rarely to be mentioned except during Lent? Are the Ten Commandments preached and upheld as the standard of conduct still to be followed? Churches who take them seriously are growing faster than those that do not.

Of course, different denominations will have different stated expectations along the spectrum of private moral behaviors. Growing up in the Bible Belt I can remember having some school friends who believed it was immoral to dance, go to the movies, or engage in any kind of work on Sunday, while other Christians felt this was acceptable and even desirable.

What is important is not necessarily where exactly a church falls on the spectrum, within reason of course, but that there are clearly stated expectations of church members. "Moral boundaries make a difference. Two out of three congregations that emphasize personal and public morality also report healthy finances and membership growth. Congregations that place less emphasis on these standards are more likely to report plateaued or declining membership."[1] Thus, a focus on moral commitment is not only critical to adding a sense of cohesion within your worshiping community, it is also significant in terms of church growth.

In addition, there are moral issues in which the public and private realms overlap significantly. It is shameful to remember that one of the great moral issues that once divided the church was slavery. The Bible was used by some to uphold the institution of slavery and by others to denounce it. Within my lifetime, Scripture has been used to support a racist stance as well as to militate against it. Here, the private becomes the public and the public is the private. How? Let me share with you my own awakening to the sin of racism.

I'll never forget the day Martin Luther King Jr. was assassinated in my home state of Tennessee. The African American students in my school staged a peaceful sit-in in the cafeteria, as some of my white classmates derided them for their actions. I will never forget the shame I felt, for the first time in my life, over the color of my white skin. I will never forget the looks on the faces of my black sisters and brothers who sat there in reverent silence.

Seventeen years later, I finally acted on the injustice I saw and the painful feelings I felt on that April afternoon in 1968. I was living a comfortable suburban life in Princeton when our daughter came home from school with an announcement about an outreach ministry in an impoverished, all-black neighborhood in Trenton, New Jersey. They were looking for people to tutor adults there at Martin House once a week, but I left the announcement in a pile of paperwork and forgot about it. Then several weeks later another announcement came and then another.

Gradually I began to suspect that there might be something God wanted to teach me in Trenton, if only I would take the first step. But I was afraid — afraid of people I didn't even know and afraid of what I might find out about myself, if I did go. Then I remembered the faces of my classmates that day in Tennessee, so many years before. And I remembered, oh how I remembered, the man who dared to dream, the man who started the march to freedom. And finally, finally I picked up my feet and started to march with him.

My perspective on the reality of life in America for all God's children was never the same after that. I soon realized that the blinders I wore were more comfortable than the truth they hid. And what is the truth? The Census Bureau tells us that the median income for whites in America is $42,439, while for African Americans, it's $25,351. Equal opportunity? The proportion of our overall population living in poverty is 12.7 percent, while for African Americans, it's an alarming 26.1 percent. That's more than one out of four. Equal opportunity? By far, the largest percentage of hate crimes in America today is against African Americans.

And what is the response of most white Americans to these realities? William Sloane Coffin says it best in his book A *Passion for the Possible*:

> For whatever reason — be it the blindness of sightless souls, the indifference of distracted people, or just plain compassion fatigue — whatever the reasons, the majority of white Americans do not feel the monstrosity of inequality so universally felt today by black Americans. The result is that racism remains bone-deep in American society.... Legal segregation, to be sure, has ended. But racial isolation has remained.[2]

Is the dream dead? Did it die on Dr. King's lips soon after his prophetic words were spoken? If so, what can we as Christian people do about it?

First of all, we can remember that there was a man before Dr. King who willingly gave *his* life for the cause of justice — Jesus of Nazareth. Jesus began his ministry with these words from the prophet Isaiah, "The Spirit of the Lord is upon me, because he has anointed me to bring good news to the poor. He has sent me to proclaim release to the captives and recovery of sight to the blind, to let the oppressed go free, to proclaim the year of the Lord's favor" (Luke 4:18–19). Jesus came to open our eyes to the realities of those held captive by an unjust system, a system based on inequality that denies the very basic fact that we are all, each and every one of us, created in the image of God. Not some of us, but all of us. The book of Genesis states, "So God created humankind in his image, in the image of God he created them; male and female he created them" (Gen. 1:27). This principle also lies at the heart of the baptismal covenant of the Episcopal Church, which commits its members to "strive for justice and peace among all people, and respect the dignity of every human being." There are no qualifiers here — *every* human being. Plain and simply, this was the dream that Dr. Martin Luther King Jr. dared to dream, a dream as old as the Bible itself.

Unfortunately the dream of racial equality, gender equality, and sexual orientation equality is one that still eludes the church. Here, the public and the private overlap in ways that can be life-giving or death-dealing to those on the receiving end of these injustices. Until I could admit that racism was alive and well in America in the year 2004, I had to ask my friends of color. Before I could admit there was gender inequality, I had to look deep into my own soul and into the ways I had allowed myself to be taken in by the system. Before I could admit that my gay and lesbian friends were routinely harassed and discriminated against, I had to ask them personally. The Rule of St. Benedict is helpful, for it is only by listening with the "ear of the heart" that we can move out of our own narrow worldviews. It is then and only then that the church will indeed become the church for all people that it proclaims itself to be.

As a sense of mission undergirded by a sense of heritage, vision, *and* moral commitment begins to take root, your congregation will be blessed with vitality that will inevitably attract newcomers to your worshiping community. How can you then welcome all the strangers God sends your way and not lose them once they have had the courage to come forward? Through hospitality to the stranger based on our Judeo-Christian heritage and the creation of a comprehensive newcomer program.

Part III

ACTION

Let mutual love continue.
Do not neglect to show hospitality to strangers,
for by doing that some have entertained angels without knowing it.
– Hebrews 13:1–2 –

Chapter 9

Hospitality Evangelism

Whether you have attracted people to your church through Fireweed Evangelism, outreach ministry, advertisements, or the simple invitation of a friend, how you extend hospitality to them once they join you for worship will significantly impact whether or not they stay. A radical hospitality that welcomes all people as angels sent by God is needed. But how are you to motivate parishioners to participate consistently in this very basic act of Christian fellowship? By helping them remember a time when they were the stranger, by raising their awareness of the distinctiveness of Christian hospitality, and by establishing a comprehensive newcomer hospitality program.

It is helpful to begin by enabling parishioners to remember a time when they were the stranger, for at different times in our lives we have all been the one standing at the threshold just hoping for a word of welcome. As children, when we enter kindergarten or first grade, we are indeed the stranger — to new surroundings, new people, and new expectations. Later, as adults, we often find ourselves in the role of stranger — in college, in the workplace, in evolving relationships, in new communities. Being the stranger is fundamental to the human experience. Simply being, living, moving, through the life cycle, we will at times find ourselves strangers in an alien land — confused, seeking, and hoping for a comforting word of reassurance.

Perhaps it is for this reason that we often find our story in the story of God's people. For our Hebrew mothers and fathers were indeed strangers in an alien land. Their physical journey from bondage in Egypt, through the wilderness, toward the promised land, parallels our own life journey — a journey with twists and unexpected turns, a journey with numerous wilderness experiences, a journey on which we are all both guests and hosts.

As we as Christian people look seriously at welcoming the stranger into our faith communities, it is critical that we connect with the experience of our Judeo-Christian forebears. Where does our story intersect with theirs? What role did hospitality play in their lives? Without such an understanding of the scriptural and theological basis for extending hospitality to the stranger, we run the risk of becoming merely another community Welcome Wagon, bringing others into our fellowship so they can begin to feel at home in new surroundings; or we may incorrectly focus on church growth in terms of new members on the rolls or new pledges on the books. What is it that marks as distinct the role of hospitality in the life of the Christian? To answer this question we must look not only at the lives of Jesus and Paul, but also at the ethos of hospitality into which they, as Jews, were born.

Hospitality in the Judeo-Christian Tradition

Within first-century Judaism, Abraham was heralded as the supreme practitioner of hospitality. In Genesis 18:1–15, Abraham reached out in hospitality to three heavenly strangers, offering them a meal of curds, milk, calf meat, and cakes. While they were eating, one gave him the seemingly impossible news that Sarah would bear a son in her old age. A few years prior to Jesus' ministry, a large monument was erected by Herod the Great on the supposed site of this meeting, not only commemorating the event, but highlighting its centrality within the Jewish tradition.

In his book *New Testament Hospitality* John Koenig states: "Undergirding the great importance attached to openness toward guests was a hope shared by many first-century Jews that God would act as bountiful host at the end of time by entertaining Israel at an endless feast."[1] Therefore, first-century Jews hoped that by welcoming the stranger themselves, God would receive them into the kingdom just as hospitably. Likewise, if they did not receive the stranger warmly, they would be received in the same way at the end of time.

This belief gives us much to consider today. What if God receives us in the same way we have received those God sends to us? At the Great Coffee Hour in the Sky will we be sitting on the side, feeling left out and alone? Or will we be welcomed with open arms by those who are already comfortably in? Will they make room for us, or not really notice that we are there? As I think of the times I have left the role of welcomer to someone else, absorbed in my own comfortable conversations, this image gives me pause to reflect.

Hospitality to the stranger was not only central to first-century Jewish and Christian belief; both religions were dependent on such hospitality for their very existence. Knowledge of the Jewish faith was perpetuated and shared by traveling pairs of Jewish teachers. These itinerant teachers, of little material means, were dependent on the hospitality of those who welcomed them into their homes. In exchange for food and lodging, they shared their Torah wisdom with family, relatives, and friends.

Jesus, a first-century Jewish teacher himself, conformed to this tradition as he went about proclaiming the word of God. He was often invited into people's homes to share his wisdom at table fellowship. For example, on his way to Jerusalem, Jesus "entered a certain village, where a woman named Martha welcomed him into her home" (Luke 10:38). As Martha prepared the meal, her sister Mary sat at Jesus' feet drinking in his wisdom. In numerous other homes throughout his ministry Jesus was welcomed and fed, even as he taught. The spreading of the teachings of Jesus was indeed dependent on the hospitality of others. As he was welcomed, fed, and nourished after his day's journey, the seeds of the church were planted. The very foundations of our Christian faith were built on those who welcomed the stranger Jesus into their homes and hearts.

Similarly, as Paul traveled about, much of his teaching was done in homes. Like the Jewish rabbis and Jesus before him, he was often dependent on the hospitality of others for providing him a place to teach the word of God. As hospitality was extended, the good news was proclaimed. Without such welcoming, the gospel message may never have spread beyond the boundaries of Palestine.

Thus, the roots of hospitality within the Judeo-Christian tradition are deep and solid, reaching back to our forebears Sarah and Abraham and spreading out to embrace those early teachers of our faith upon whom the very existence of Christianity is dependent. Over the centuries, this hospitality has been offered again and again in the name of Christ.

In my great-grandfather's autobiography, he tells of a Southern religious revival held in 1879 where strangers were welcomed, much as they were in Palestine, with kindness, food, and lodging.

> The chief vehicle of interest and attention for the summer was the big meeting, held frequently under a brush arbor. Literally thousands of people came, came with every mode of conveyance. Every class and condition of people was represented. The utmost courtesy, good will and neighborliness prevailed. Any stranger that wanted to attend the meeting could get all he wanted to eat, a place to sleep and the kindest of treatment.[2]

Not only was hospitality extended in this nineteenth-century meeting, but it was extended to "every class and condition of people."

As we discuss welcoming the stranger into our faith communities today, we need to address the question, Who is the stranger? Will every class and condition of people be equally welcome in our churches? Who was the stranger in Jesus' day, and who is the stranger for us now? In defining the stranger, we can begin to define our role in welcoming those persons sent to us by God.

Fireweed Hospitality

In the movie *Sister Act*, its star Whoopi Goldberg, a raucous nightclub singer and mistress in Reno, witnesses a murder. As a result, her own life is in danger. For protection, the police decide she should live in a convent, a most unlikely hideout. She is taken to St. Katherine's Convent in San Francisco and directed to the Mother Superior's study. Before the Mother Superior enters, a monsignor informs her of Whoopi's predicament. The Mother Superior agrees to accept Whoopi as a member of the convent, until she opens the door and sees her. There sits Whoopi, wearing a gold lamé coat, a purple-sequined outfit, and a profusion of jewelry. The Mother Superior gasps and shuts the door. The monsignor reminds her, in not-so-gentle tones, "You have taken a vow of hospitality to all in need." With a straight face, the Mother Superior replies, "I lied."

How often do we, upon seeing the strangers who come our way, say somewhere in our heart of hearts, "I lied — I lied when I took my baptismal vows and promised to seek and serve Christ in all persons and to respect the dignity of every human being"? This promise is found in the rite of Holy Baptism used by the Episcopal Church, while other denominations use similar wording. And although most of us would never consciously admit it, our behavior may nonetheless at times bear witness to this reality.

As one church was preparing for its annual Christmas bazaar, one harmless, disheveled parishioner who was mentally ill walked back to the kitchen and offered to help with the food preparation. The woman was new in the community and eager to give to the church in a way that she could. A church worker for the bazaar told me in disbelief that a staff member had advised her to usher the woman out, because she was homeless and unbalanced. To be sure, some strangers may represent a possible danger to others and should be dealt with accordingly; however, this was not the case here. We do not expect this response to the stranger in a church that preaches love of neighbor and the inclusivity of God's love, yet it happens more often than any of us like to think.

What separates us as a Christian community is precisely how we welcome those who may be unwelcome in other settings. The Letter of James clearly states this central Christian belief.

> For if a person with gold rings and in fine clothes comes into your assembly, and if a poor person in dirty clothes also comes in, and if you take notice of the one wearing the fine clothes and say, "Have a seat here, please," while to the one who is poor you say, "Stand there," or "Sit at my feet," have you not made distinctions among yourselves, and become judges with evil thoughts? Listen, my beloved brothers and sisters. Has not God chosen the poor in the world to be rich in faith and to be heirs of the kingdom that he has promised to those who love him? (James 2:2–5)

It is clear throughout Scripture that we are to extend radical hospitality to all strangers. How easy it is to welcome the young, nicely dressed family, with children in tow, who can offer their time to committee work and various church functions. But how about the many other strangers God sends our way? How about the elderly, the physically or the mentally disabled, the unwed couple living together, the couple recently married after a publicly known extramarital affair, the person with AIDS, the homosexual or lesbian couple, the person recently released from prison, the white-collar criminal recently indicted on insider trading charges? How will we welcome these people? Will we, like the Mother Superior in *Sister Act*, turn away from our vows and say, "I lied"?

Reaching out to those individuals who have been wounded or hurt lies at the heart of Fireweed Evangelism. Those who have consistently not been welcomed by others are injured by this neglect. Whether they have been ostracized because of who they are or what they have done, what marks us as Christians is that we reach out to these people and welcome them with open arms. Once these strangers find their way to us, God calls us to engage in what I call Fireweed Hospitality, a radical hospitality inclusive of all God's children, particularly those who have been hurt because they are not welcome in other settings.

Fireweed Hospitality is deeply rooted in the Christian tradition. Jesus' hospitality to sinners and the unacceptable was a hallmark of his ministry. He regularly dined with tax collectors, the pariahs of his day, causing much trouble for himself, as well as for the word he was proclaiming (Mark 2:15–17; Luke 15:1–2). How could anyone who dined with tax collectors have a message that was worth receiving? Moreover, when the scribes and Pharisees brought the adulterous woman to Jesus, he did not condemn her but sided with her against those who found her unacceptable, again causing trouble for himself (John 8:2–11).

When Jesus read from the scroll of the prophet Isaiah, in the synagogue in Nazareth, he made it clear that his ministry was for everyone, especially the poor and oppressed, many of whom were women. The most oppressed of women were widows, because they had no standing before the law, no one to provide for them, and almost no means of livelihood. Jesus shows concern for and acceptance of widows in the story of the widow's mite (Luke 21:1–4; Mark 12:41–44); in his teaching regarding the scribes who "devour widows' houses" (Luke 20:45–47; Mark 12:38–40); in raising to life the only son of the widow of Nain (Luke 7:11–17); and in his teaching that Elijah was sent to a widow at Zarephath (Luke 4:25–27).[3]

Throughout his ministry, Jesus showed acceptance of many of society's outcasts. The woman who had been bleeding for twelve years was ritually unclean according to Jewish law (Lev. 15:19–30), yet Jesus touched her and healed her (Matt. 9:20–22; Mark 5:24–34; Luke 8:43–48). In healing the Gerasenes man possessed with demons and the ten people with leprosy, Jesus again touched those who were feared and ostracized by society (Luke 8:26–39; Luke 17:11–19). In his willingness to engage in conversation with the Samaritan woman at the well, Jesus broke several Jewish customs (John 4:5–30). Normally, not only would a Jew not address a Samaritan, but a man would not speak to a woman in public, especially if the man was a rabbi.

As Jesus welcomed the outcast with open arms, so too have others followed in his footsteps. Where would Christianity be today if Ananias had not welcomed the outcast Paul into his faith community? Paul, who had openly persecuted Christians, was hardly an acceptable stranger of his day. In *New Testament Hospitality* John Koenig writes: "Paul's history as a believer begins with the residential disciple Ananias and the community at Damascus to which he belongs. Without this local church's courageous welcoming of its persecutor, there would have been no Christian Paul."[4] Furthermore, at the beginning of Paul's missionary career, his associates feared that he was a secret agent of the Jerusalem authorities. Even so, Barnabas, a member of the community, recommended him to the apostles (Acts 9:26–30). In the language of hospitality, Barnabas welcomed this volatile newcomer into the mainstream of the church's life. It is difficult to think of Paul as a newcomer, yet he was — and an unacceptable one at that. He was volatile, on the fringe, and suspected of being a secret agent. Yet what gifts did this stranger bring, not only to those who welcomed him, but to all of Christendom?

In the world of nature, twentieth-century poet Mary Sammons Patton sees this reality revealed in her poem "To a Bulb":

> Who would ever think
> To look at you,
> You brownish, ugly, shriveled thing
> That you hold within the depths
> Of you
> The very heart of Spring![5]

We often find the heart of spring, the gift of life, in the places we least expect to find it. In *Sister Act*, the very person the Mother Superior did not want to welcome ultimately became the answer to the prayers of an ailing

inner-city congregation. Whoopi used her gifts of singing and teaching to
give the convent choir a new voice, a new sound, a new spirit. As new life
filled their lungs, new life was breathed into the dwindling congregation.
Gradually, the pews began to fill, as the shriveled bulb burst forth into
colorful song.

Those who offer Fireweed Hospitality to the stranger often receive
far more than they give. How is it that those we welcome, even re-
luctantly, often welcome us in turn? As guests become hosts and hosts
become guests, God's work within the sacred relationship of hospitality
often becomes manifest.

Guest/Host Reversals

When we make the decision to welcome all strangers, we become a link
in the chain of hospitality that reaches back through Sarah and Abraham,
through Jesus and Ananias, through countless Christians throughout the
centuries. When we make the decision to extend hospitality to another
in the name of Christ, we enter into a sacred relationship where God is
present. "For where two or three are gathered in my name, I am there
among them" (Matt. 18:20).

Jesus Christ, the Word made flesh, is the revelation of God in our midst.
Jesus is the Word of God. The Word is God's ongoing self-communication,
God's reaching out to humanity, God's revelation. In *The Word of God
and Pastoral Care*, Howard Stone writes: "God addresses us in the word;
in the word we encounter the One who is indeed with us. This meeting
of God and person in the word has about it a sense of call — the call into
relationship."[6]

When we are called into relationship with the stranger, we are called to
be hosts in the truest sense of the word. Margaret Guenther's *Holy Listening*
notes that the German words for "host" perhaps convey this depth of
meaning better than the English. *Gastgeber* means "the guest-giver," the
one who gives to guests, and *Gastfreundschaft* denotes a guest-friendship,
the special friendship that is shown by hosts to guests. As we welcome the
stranger, we are called to be bestowers of such guest-friendship, reflecting
the warm hospitality shown by the host at the heavenly banquet.[7] As

we are called into relationship with another, we are called to extend this special friendship. As we reach out in the name of Christ in this act of friendship, we can become both bearers and receivers of the word of God.

It is the awareness of the presence of God within such relationships that enables us to be not only hosts, but guests. For this to occur when we enter into dialogue with the stranger, we need to participate in mutual listening. We must be willing not only to give in the name of Christ, but to receive in the name of Christ as well, for what often comes to us in and through the other's utterances is nothing less than God's word for us.

This guest/host reversal is vividly depicted in the story of Abraham's welcoming of the three heavenly strangers in Genesis 18:1–15. Abraham runs from his tent to meet them, bows down, and then offers them water, rest, and food. As they are eating the meal prepared for them, one of the strangers reveals God's word to Sarah and Abraham. Sarah is to have a son in her old age. In reflecting on this passage from Genesis, moreover, the author of Hebrews wrote: "Let mutual love continue. Do not neglect to show hospitality to strangers, for by doing that some have entertained angels without knowing it" (Heb. 13:1–2). Just as these angels were God's messengers to Sarah and Abraham, the angels God sends to us today are God's messengers.

A similar guest/host reversal is found in Luke's Gospel following the passion narrative, when two people on the road to Emmaus encounter a stranger. They act as host to him, telling their story of the death of the Messiah; then they listen as the stranger shares his knowledge of Scripture regarding the role of the messiah (Luke 24:13–27). As they come to the village to which they are going, the stranger walks ahead as if he is going on. "But they urged him strongly, saying, 'Stay with us, because it is almost evening and the day is now nearly over'" (Luke 24:29). It is through this act of welcoming the stranger into their home for the breaking of bread that they learn it is Jesus to whom they are speaking. The hosts to the stranger become the guests of Christ. As guests, they are able to hear God's word for them. If they had never reached out to this stranger, how different their lives would have been.

The host as receiver of God's gifts from the stranger is lyrically portrayed in an old Gaelic rune:

I saw a stranger yestreen;
I put food in the eating place,
Drink in the drinking place,
Music in the listening place;
And in the blessed name of the Triune
he blessed myself and my house,
my cattle and my dear ones.
        And the lark said in her song
                often, often, often,
        Goes the Christ in the stranger's guise;
                Often, often, often,
        Goes the Christ in the stranger's guise.

Welcoming the Christ in the stranger's guise, furthermore, is deeply rooted in our biblical tradition. In addition to the encounter with Christ as the stranger on the road to Emmaus is the narration of Christ's appearance as a gardener to Mary Magdalene as she stands weeping outside his tomb (John 20:11–18; see the illustration on page 147). Had she not spoken with this stranger, she would have never known that, in fact, it was the risen Christ to whom she was speaking. In Matthew 25, Jesus tells us that such instances are not restricted to his resurrection appearances, but occur in everyday life. In the parable of the sheep and the goats, the righteous ask him, "When was it that we saw you a stranger and welcomed you?" And he answered them, "Truly I tell you, just as you did it to one of the least of these who are members of my family, you did it to me" (Matt. 25:31–46). Hospitality to the stranger was a hallmark of the kingdom of God in Jesus' day, just as it is today — "often, often, often goes the Christ in the stranger's guise."

Many times in my own life I have offered hospitality to the stranger and have been surprised by God's word for me, revealed through that person. Regardless of how often this happens, I am always filled with wonder when it does. Such guest/host reversals occurred frequently when I was working at Martin House. I believed I was called there to teach, but I soon learned that I was there not so much to teach as to learn, not so much to change as to be changed. The teaching was more of a dialogue in which both parties had much to give and to be given.

I remember vividly one morning when one of my students was particularly agitated. She was a middle-aged woman who had been homeless most of her adult life. I took Emma into another room, where used clothing was stored for resale in the community. She stood in the midst of the musty boxes piled high, in clothes she had worn for two weeks. Her eyes were often glazed and seemed to be searching in a far-off place, but they were very alert and alive at that moment. She told me over and over that someday people would not judge her by her outward appearance, but would see her for the type of person she was and for the type of heart she had. She just stood there, patting her heart, repeating these words to me. At that moment, my eye was drawn to a small glass ball that hung from a chain around her neck. It was about the size of a dime and contained one tiny seed. "Emma, what is this?" I asked. "That's a mustard seed," she replied. "That's what keeps me going, and keeps me knowing, that someday things will be different."

Emma lived out the message of Jesus to his disciples in Matthew 17, putting it at the center of her life. When the disciples were unable to heal a boy with epilepsy, they asked Jesus privately, "Why could we not cast it out?" He said to them, "Because of your little faith. For truly I tell you, if you have faith the size of a mustard seed, you will say to this mountain, 'Move from here to there,' and it will move; and nothing will be impossible for you" (Matt. 17:19–21).

I learned as much about faith from that one conversation with Emma as I could have learned from reading books or listening to sermons. God's word for me was clear, as I learned what it meant to receive the word of God from someone I thought was there to learn from me. It is particularly in extending Fireweed Hospitality to the oppressed, the disenfranchised, or the wounded that I have been blessed by the word of God revealed to me through them. When we receive another in the name of Christ and believe in mutual listening for the word of God, we will be surprised again and again by the many angels God sends our way. For as Henri Nouwen writes, "Reaching out to strangers is not just reaching out to the long row of people who are so obviously needy — in need of food, clothing and of many forms of care — but also a reaching out to the promises they are bringing with them as gifts to their host."[8]

To be open to receive these gifts, we must be willing to leave our own safe place and to let ourselves be guided. Abba James of the desert knew it was easier to be the host than the guest when he wrote, "It is better to receive hospitality than to offer it." Those who find it easier to reach out to others than to let someone reach out to them would do well to heed his words, for without the willingness to let God work within our encounters with strangers, we will miss the gifts they bring to us.

This guest/host reversal and the gifts imparted within the sacred relationship based on hospitality are contained within the Greek word for "hospitality," *philoxenia,* used in the New Testament. This word refers not only to a love and acceptance of strangers, but to a delight in the whole guest/host relationship, in the mysterious reversals and gains for both parties that may occur. For those who believe, this delight is fueled by the expectation that God will play a role in the guest/host encounter.[9] It is such mysterious reversals that both delight and instruct those who are open to receive God's word from the Christ in the stranger's guise.

Reaching out to the strangers who have found their way into your church begins with a ministry of presence, a willingness to meet them where they are and to listen to them with an understanding that God is the unseen party in all your encounters. Beyond that, however, a comprehensive newcomer program is needed, or these very same people will "fall through the cracks" and you may lose the many gifts they bring with them for your church community.

Chapter 10

Components of
Successful Hospitality Programs

At a newcomer workshop I was giving one year, I began with my usual question, "What led you to this particular church?" One couple related that they had stumbled upon the church quite by accident. "Shortly after we moved here, we saw a sign for another congregation in this denomination, St. Mary's in the Field. We asked about it and heard it was a friendly, caring place, so we decided to give it a try. On the way to St. Mary's, our car suddenly ran out of gas directly in front of this church! The ten o'clock service was about to begin, so we just locked the car and went in. I don't know whether it was an act of God or what, but we've been coming here ever since and we couldn't be happier."

To be sure, people may first enter the doors of our church for a variety of reasons — some quite unanticipated. Regardless of how newcomers find their way to us, once they arrive it is our call to extend hospitality to them in the name of Christ. This involves more than just offering an initial welcome. As we welcome others into the body of Christ, it is important that we engage in story-listening. In addition, intentional follow-up through a newcomer program is essential.

Research has shown that effective programs vary, depending on the size of the congregation. In determining size, it is most helpful to look at Average Sunday Attendance (ASA), rather than members on the rolls. Keith B. Brown, who writes on congregational development, divides churches into five groups based on their ASA: Family Congregations with an ASA of 1–75, Pastoral Congregations with an ASA of 76–140, Transitional Congregations with an ASA of 141–225, Program Congregations with an ASA of 226–400, and Resource Congregations with an ASA of 400 and over.[1]

However, some congregations *function* more like one with a higher or lower ASA. For example, some pastoral congregations function more like family-size churches. If you are unclear on this point, check with recent newcomers and ask about their experience of your congregation upon first attending. This will provide valuable insight into your functional size and how your church system actually works.

It is important to know that churches with an ASA of less than 150 tend to get smaller when left to their own devices, while churches over 150 tend to get larger. Our culture seems to support larger congregations. Therefore, pastoral- and family-size churches are at risk. Transitional-size churches are also at risk, but for a different reason. Recent research has shown that churches on the cusp of moving from pastoral- to program-size have the most difficulty, i.e., the system puts up the most resistance to growth. If you are a member of a transitional church, see Alice Mann's excellent book *Raising the Roof: The Pastoral-to-Program Size Transition.*[2]

Successful hospitality ministries in transitional, program, and resource churches are similar and will be addressed first. Alterations to this more comprehensive undertaking will then be discussed in light of the needs of family- and pastoral-size churches. Successful programs differ from church to church, but at their heart lie two key elements: a willingness of members to offer hospitality through story-listening, and lay ownership and involvement in the program. To enable these two elements to occur, laity need a theological background for hospitality ministry, consciousness raising about possible newcomer needs, and a chance to develop their own program. Moreover, effective newcomer programs contain a number of other key components: corporate prayer, greeting, tracking, calling, orienting, and integrating newcomers handled in a systematic yet caring way. It is to these components that I now turn.

Corporate Prayer

Praying for newcomers each and every Sunday is a wonderful way not only to help all guests feel welcomed and wanted in your church, but also to raise the consciousness of members about the reality of new people worshiping with them. There is an excellent welcoming prayer that can be used for this purpose in *Women's Uncommon Prayers:*

> Holy Spirit living within us, guide our hearts and minds as we welcome today all those who worship with us at N. Give us discerning hearts so that every one who crosses our threshold feels welcomed in the spirit of your love. Help us to recognize each person as an individual sent by you who will enrich our lives. And most of all, O God, let this be a place of love and acceptance of all your children; in the name of your Child, our Savior, Jesus Christ. Amen.[3]

In addition, encourage members to pray regularly for all those who are seeking a church home, as well as for those who have taken the step to seek out your congregation.

Hospitality Ministers

It is important for program, transitional, and resource churches to have greeters at each entrance of the church on Sunday mornings. Since the word "greeter" can imply a kind of glad-hand approach, I prefer to use the term "hospitality minister," for such a person is far more than a mere welcomer in the secular sense. Hospitality ministers may be commissioned at a worship service, for such an offering of one's time is indeed a lay ministry.[4] It is best to schedule these lay ministers for four weeks in a row. By the second or third Sunday, they will be familiar with who is new and who is not. In addition, they will be able to recognize newcomers who may be attending for their second or third visits.

In liturgical churches it is helpful for hospitality ministers to ask whether guests are familiar with the liturgy. If not, it is best to seat them next to parishioners who can help them find their way through the service. A humorous story about Ronald and Nancy Reagan, written by Michael K. Deaver, highlights the difficulties encountered by guests who are not familiar with the service of Holy Communion in an Episcopal Church.

> The Episcopal service is somewhat more formal, with kneeling and a common chalice and considerably more ritual. This kind of Mass was very foreign to the Reagans and within minutes after we were inside the church they kept sending nervous glances my way. They were turning pages of the

prayer book as fast as they could, and I was handing them loose pages to help them keep up.

Nancy whispered to me in a mildly frantic voice, "Mike, what are we supposed to do?" I explained the ceremony as quickly and as confidently as I could: how we would walk to the altar and kneel, the minister would pass by with the wine (the blood of Christ), and the wafers (the body of Christ). He would bless them and keep moving.

The president, who as most people know [had] a slight hearing problem, leaned toward us but picked up little of what I was saying.

We started toward the altar and halfway down the aisle I felt Nancy Reagan clutch my arm. In front of us, all I could see were people crossing themselves and genuflecting. "Mike!" She hissed. "Are those people drinking out of the same cup?"

You have to remember that Nancy is the daughter of a doctor. I said, "It's all right. They'll come by with the wafers first. Then, when the chalice reaches you, dip the bread in the cup and that is perfectly all right. You won't have to put your lips to the cup."

The president said, "What? What?"

Nancy said, "Ron, just do exactly as I do."

Unknown to me, the church had made its wafers out of unleavened bread, which gave them the look and hardness of Jewish matzoh. Nancy selected a square of bread, and when the chalice came by she dipped hers...and dropped it. The square sank in the wine. She looked at me with huge eyes.

By then the trays had reached the president. Very calmly, and precisely, he picked up a piece of unleavened bread and dropped it in the wine. I watched the minister move on, shaking his head, staring at these blobs of gunk in his wine.

Nancy was relieved to leave the church. The president was chipper as he stepped into the sunlight, satisfied that the service had gone quite well.[5]

Those of us who are long-time members of liturgical churches need to be reminded of how bewildering such worship can be for those who are attending for the first time. Just as Nancy Reagan was "relieved to leave the church," how many guests are relieved to leave our churches after fumbling through leaflets, prayer books, and hymnals? Imagine, too, their confusion concerning the numerous traditions that are distinct within such denominations. It is helpful for such churches to raise the consciousness of parishioners, encouraging them to willingly volunteer their assistance if the person next to them seems to be confused.

After the service, hospitality ministers can return to the doors, inviting all newcomers to attend coffee hour or adult education events. During such events, it is important for all parishioners to wear nametags. A board with grooves can be used to alphabetize pin-on nametags with plastic jackets. Another method is to use nametags in plastic jackets with a string attached, to be worn around the neck. These tags can be hung on hooks, with all the As on one hook, all the Bs on another, and so on. Whatever method is used, it is best if newcomer tags are of a different color from those of church members so that they can be easily located. In addition, it is helpful for the nametag table or board to be staffed by two parishioners, enabling them to greet new people warmly, as well as to introduce them to members of the church. Information about upcoming church events can also be kept near the nametags and given to all guests.

At St. Columba's in Washington, D.C., rather than printing the familiar reminder in their Sunday bulletin about coffee hour following the service, they write: "There is hospitality after every service — coffee in the Great Hall after all services and iced tea in the Common after 10:15." What a different focus is provided by the statement that it is hospitality that is really being offered, not merely coffee or tea. Such a notice also serves as a valuable reminder to established church members.

Unfortunately, it can happen during coffee hour that new people are left standing alone while church members talk to one another. The pastor of a church in California illustrates a solution to this problem. "We organized 'secret hosts.' As the crowd moves from the sanctuary into the coffee hour after worship, these three or four couples watch for people who are standing alone, talking to nobody."[6] After spotting people who are standing alone, these secret hosts accompany them into coffee hour, visit with the guests, and then introduce them to other parishioners. This helps break the cycle of unintentional exclusivity that can develop in parishes.

Act of Friendship Tablet and Lay Calling

In any hospitality program it is critical to obtain the name and address of every guest, every Sunday morning. In a large church, even the pew card method, hospitality ministers at the doors, and well-staffed nametag areas cannot secure the names of all guests. To do so, the most fail-proof, least intrusive method I have found is the use of an Act of Friendship Tablet, passed during the announcements in the worship service (page 141).

A friendship tablet serves two different functions in program, transitional, and resource churches. First, it supplies the church with an immediate list of all newcomers in attendance that day. Second, it gives people in each pew a chance to know who the newcomers are and to welcome them accordingly. The concept of a friendship tablet may seem too "folksy" to some congregations when it is first mentioned. However, even well-established liturgical churches have found that the merits far outweigh the brief time it takes to become accustomed to its use.

At the end of the Sunday morning service, the Act of Friendship Tablet can be used to compile a list of all first-time guests. It is best for each one to receive a call from a lay visitor that same afternoon. Herb Miller in *How to Build a Magnetic Church* gives these statistics: "When lay persons make fifteen-minute visits to the homes of first-time worship visitors within thirty-six hours, 85 percent of them return the following week. Make this home visit within seventy-two hours, and 60 percent of them return. Make it seven days later, and 15 percent will return."[7] By waiting merely one week to make our initial visit, we risk losing 70 percent of the strangers God sends our way. *Interestingly, this research also found that if clergy make this call, rather than laypersons, the results are each cut in half.* Thus, an effective lay calling system is indeed the cornerstone of an effective newcomer program.

It is important to keep in mind that growth is not the objective. Rather, offering hospitality to all who come our way is the goal. When hospitality is not immediately extended beyond an in-church welcome, the strangers God sends our way may be lost. These lost strangers are God's children, God's lost gift to us. These lost strangers are our responsibility. To meet this responsibility requires an effective, responsive calling system.

At Trinity Cathedral in San Francisco, hospitality ministers follow specific guidelines for calling. "If invited in, they never stay longer than fifteen minutes. 'Be bright, be brief, be gone' is the rule." For these brief visits it is best not to telephone in advance, because the answer is nearly always, "I'm fine. A visit isn't necessary."

Hospitality ministers for a given Sunday can serve as both greeters and callers. Grace Episcopal Church in Paducah, Kentucky, uses this method. On Sunday afternoon, the Sunday morning hospitality ministers take a nicely wrapped loaf of bread to the newcomer's home. If the person is not there, they simply leave the bread with a short note attached that includes the caller's name and telephone number. Bradley Tate, a hospitality minister in this program, stated in an interview: "It is much easier to knock on a stranger's door if you have something like bread to give them. It gives you a purpose for being there, other than merely saying, 'We're glad you came!' It is also symbolic of offering them the body of Christ, which adds a completely different dimension to the visit."

In her book *Leaven for Our Lives,* Alice Downs shares the spirituality involved in baking a loaf of bread, as well as in giving the loaf to another. She writes, "Every loaf of bread offers the promise of welcome and hospitality. The promise is contained in the living process of fermentation that works on the mixture of flour, water, and salt. When Abraham and Sarah were surprised by a visit from three strangers, messengers of God, Sarah baked bread quickly in order to offer them hospitality (Gen. 18). We bakers welcome the hope of a new creation each time we bake a new loaf."[8]

A calling system is most successful if it is designed to meet the needs of both the newcomer and the lay caller. Consideration of both parties involved is important. If possible, assign hospitality ministers to guests in or near their own neighborhoods, giving them as much available information as possible about the person to be visited. Supplying the caller with a loaf of bread as well as information about the church to give the newcomer can also increase the comfort level of both parties.

From the information on the Act of Friendship Tablet, the hospitality ministry chairperson can develop a record of all newcomer visits. Storing this information in a computer is best, but for those churches that prefer the "notebook" method, a sample record-keeping form for this purpose is given on page 150. In addition to providing information for afternoon visits by hospitality ministers, the friendship tablet can be helpful in a number of other ways. For example, after one visit to Madison Street United Methodist Church in Clarksville, Tennessee, newcomers begin receiving that church's newsletter. "If you breathe, you get our weekly newsletter," stated the director of music ministries at the church. "It makes a difference when newcomers immediately begin receiving weekly reminders of church events," he said. If a newcomer does not attend for six to eight weeks in a row, the person's name is taken off the mailing list. If the person suddenly comes back, he or she is immediately added to the list once again. After a second visit, he telephones newcomers with information about the church's choir program, which serves the needs of people from age five to adult. If the guests have school-age children, they also receive a call from the director of religious education. Using this system, the church has grown by more than one hundred members per year in the last two years.

After a newcomer's third visit, a welcoming letter from the clergy can be mailed (page 142), along with a parish brochure (pages 139–40) and a Newcomer Information Sheet (page 143) to be returned to the church. Because it is important for clergy to have personal contact with as many newcomers as possible, a clergy call is also desirable at this time.

In addition, some churches may want to assign a "shepherd" to each newcomer. Shepherds should be parishioners who know their way around the congregation and are willing to shepherd a new member for at least two years. Shepherds can introduce newcomers to as many people as possible and invite them to sit with them at various church functions. Moreover, shepherds may want to call their newcomers once a month just to see how they are doing. Likewise, clergy or the hospitality ministry chairperson may want to check in regularly with the shepherds to see if they are comfortable in their role with newcomers.

When hospitality ministers and shepherds are secure in their roles, they often begin to claim the authority that is theirs as lay ministers, thereby fostering a feeling of shared ministry between clergy and laity. Not only are clergy and laity performing similar functions in welcoming the new member, but there is also a feeling of shared ministry with regard to the pastoral care of newcomers. These lay ministers can often share valuable insights about newcomers with clergy, increasing clergy awareness of special areas of need. Meeting the needs of hospitality ministers in their functions as both greeters and callers, as well as the needs of shepherds, is not only critical to the success of a church's hospitality ministry, but is equally important in developing the concept of lay ministry within a parish.

Orienting and Integrating New Members

In addition to providing these personal contacts with new people, effective newcomer programs educate new members about the parish while simultaneously educating the parish about new people. Trinity Church in Princeton, New Jersey, successfully uses several different methods for this mutual education. It offers a newcomer forum in the fall, a newcomer party at the rector's home in the spring, and a monthly article in the church newsletter. Because people respond to a variety of activities, this church finds it helpful to offer at least two newcomer events with differing formats throughout the year. Each activity serves a distinct purpose and meets a variety of needs, therefore reaching a broad range of people.

The first of these, the Sunday morning newcomer forum, is led by the laity of Trinity Church. Committee chairpersons give a brief overview of their particular areas, with most of the time devoted to a question-and-answer period. A handout describing church programs is also provided. At such events, it is important to stress that newcomers do not have to become involved in any of these activities. The information should not be given for recruitment purposes, but rather to stimulate discussion and questions about various church offerings. Trinity's newcomer party in the spring is designed to greet newcomers on a more informal basis. Because this event is not held on Sunday morning, it attracts additional new people who attend weekday and early Sunday services. In planning your own events, make sure that lay leaders attend the party and forum, because it is important to provide an environment in which the parish as a whole can share the responsibility of welcoming new members. In addition, it is best if as many parishioners as possible staff the nametag area on Sunday morning.

Even though these responsibilities are shared, the parish at large is often unaware of the number of new people who are becoming a part of their worshiping community. To address this need, Trinity publishes Newcomer News (page 151) in their church newsletter. In addition to the names and addresses of new members, a paragraph is included that informs the parish about newcomer events, suggests that people call newcomers in their neighborhoods, or reminds parishioners to be especially aware of new people during the summer months. This consciousness-raising effort is well received, and many parishioners note with surprise the large number of new members.

In some denominations, there is a question as to when someone actually becomes a member of the local church. For example, (a) is it only after confirmation or reception, or (b) is it anyone who pledges or gives regularly to the church? In most congregations, there is an unwritten rule that the answer is "b," yet this is usually not formally acknowledged.

To address this question a New Member Dedication Litany can be used during a worship service (page 145). Newcomers are often quite willing to participate in this special part of the service, which can be followed by a celebratory potluck lunch complete with icebreakers, balloons, and flowers. This ritualized acknowledgment of new members often leads them to deeper involvement in their church community. I have often used the litany in conjunction with Invite-a-Friend Sunday, increasing the focus on new members and new life.

Events such as these are invaluable tools in helping new members feel at home; yet this is only the beginning of what it means to be hospitable in the Christian sense. True hospitality within a church setting must reach to the deeper parts of our faith. True integration is not only integration into one church, but integration into the body of Christ.

Integration into the body of Christ begins at baptism, an ideal time to integrate new families into the life of the congregation. Many couples will seek to reconnect with a church when they desire to have their child baptized; yet they often fail to return following this special event. Guild of the Christ Child is a wonderful program with a two-year follow-up for parents of the newly baptized.[9] It contains letters and cards to send to the new parents at anniversaries, keeping them connected to the church. To deepen this connection, each newcomer couple can be assigned a lay sponsor who actually attends the baptismal preparation with the couple. The sponsor then attends the baptism and the party afterward, if there is one. This sponsor then becomes the newcomer's shepherd as described in the previous section. The importance of this program to successful integration of new families into the church cannot be overstated.

To further integrate new members into the life of the congregation, a strong adult education program designed especially for them is needed, providing a deeper sense of community and commitment. All Saints Church in Pasadena, California, has developed a covenant program to address this need. The purpose of the program is to prepare adults for confirmation in the Episcopal Church and for membership in All Saints. A person who decides not to be confirmed may become a general member of All Saints. The difference between this and other new-member incorporation programs is that it has a twofold structure. It is held once a week on nine weeknight evenings from 7:30 p.m. to 9:30 p.m. The first hour is used for a forum presentation; the second hour is for small covenant group meetings. On the Saturday before confirmation, a Quiet Day is held from 8:30 a.m. to 3:00 p.m. with a covenant dinner at 6:00 p.m.

The small covenant group meetings, held immediately after the forum presentation, focus on spiritual issues and enable participants to know one another on a deeper level. The covenant groups are small and led by the laity. Once the initial welcoming is over, there must be a structure designed specifically for new people, enabling them to come together in a more intimate environment. All Saints' introductory letter to covenant groups describes this focus in greater detail (page 152).

As the strangers we welcome on Sunday morning become active members of our congregations, it is important that we not assume they are well integrated after the first year. In a large church, the one-year anniversary for a newcomer is a critical one. For this reason, it is best if newcomers can be contacted by a member of the clergy or by the hospitality ministry chairperson at the one-year mark.

Newcomer Programs in the Small Church

In family- and pastoral-size churches, a conscious effort on behalf of new-comers is still necessary, although it need not be as elaborate as that in program, transitional, or resource churches. For example, the dynamics are quite different in a family church. To implement a hospitality ministry effectively in this setting, it is important to understand what those dynamics are. Family churches with fifty members or fewer often operate as a single-cell unit that can be "so warm you can't get in," as Alice Mann describes it. In churches of this size, there is generally one person who introduces new people to parish leaders. Newcomers are often screened in this way and then adopted one-by-one into the church family.

In a family church, spiritual formation of the key welcomers is necessary to fostering Christian openness. They need to be conscious of their role in welcoming new members. They need to be sensitive about filling in the newcomer on what people are talking and laughing about. They need to be aware that in the powerful desire of some churches to stay small, there can be a kind of cruel homogeneity that can be less than welcoming. Without such a spiritual awareness, lay leaders of family churches may exclude people without being aware of the dynamics at play.

Clergy of family parishes interested in building up the membership of their churches might keep in mind that the movement from family- to pastoral-size congregations is difficult to make. Those attached to the single-cell dynamic of a family parish are there because they like it that way. Powerful emotions and language can follow even an expressed desire for growth. In addition, the expectation in churches of this size is often that the clergyperson function more as a chaplain rather than as a trainer for lay ministry. Thus, training of the laity for newcomer ministry should begin with education for the parish about the importance of their role in hospitality ministry. Another factor to consider is that codependent relationships can develop between clergy and laity, as the late Edwin Friedman pointed out in his book on family and church systems, *Generation to Generation*.[10] Thus, a newcomer strategy in family parishes is to educate the laity about their role in welcoming new members, to attend to the spiritual formation of the key welcomers, to replace them if necessary after prayerful consideration, to add new helpers as growth requires, and to be aware of possible codependent relationships between clergy and laity.

In pastoral-size parishes, most of the basic elements of the program outlined here can be implemented. A hospitality ministry chairperson is needed in these congregations to handle the administrative duties. However, a structured hospitality committee is not necessary. Instead, a more flexible strategy is best, with the clergy assuming a central role and selecting three or four helpers, based on their gifts for hospitality ministry. Rather than a structured committee, it is best to think of this group as a team. Use of an Act of Friendship Tablet is not necessary in family- or pastoral-size churches. Visitors are easier to spot, and a hospitality minister at the door can obtain names before and after the service. Moreover, one newcomer event per year is usually adequate.

Regardless of size, every church that undertakes a hospitality ministry needs to be clear about the ultimate goal of such ministry. The goal is for new members to become Christ's conscious agents in the setting of their daily lives — at work, at home, in the community, in the area of citizenship, in leisure activities — as well as within the church. Without this vision for mission in the world, a church's hospitality program can be centered inward toward the needs of the individual congregation rather than outward toward the needs of the world. Success is most likely if this vision is at the heart of a church's hospitality program and is articulated throughout its development.

The prophet Isaiah tells us, "Enlarge the site of your tent, and let the curtains of your habitations be stretched out; do not hold back; lengthen your cords and strengthen your stakes" (Isa. 54:2). For churches that want to "enlarge the site of their tent," an effective hospitality program is necessary. For parishioners to "not hold back," consciousness raising and education are needed concerning our unique call as Christians to hospitality ministry. As we "lengthen our cords" and "strengthen our stakes," it is we who will be strengthened and enriched, both as a church and as individuals. For it is "through the stranger our view of self, of world, of God is deepened and expanded. Through the stranger we are given a chance to find ourselves. And through the stranger, God finds us and offers us the gift of wholeness."[11]

Chapter 11

Gift Discernment Retreat

Session 1
Letting Your Light Shine

Materials Needed: Nametags, newsprint and markers, copies of the song "This Little Light of Mine," individual candles for each participant with drip holders, matches

Handouts: "Scripture Passages about Community" (page 154)

Quotation: "You are the light of the world." (Matt. 5:14)

1. Seat participants in groups of no more than eight, with a facilitator for each group. Each group should have their own newsprint and marker.

2. Give the following talk or something similar:

"This little light of mine, I'm going to let it shine." In the words of this simple childhood song lies a great truth, yet one that eludes many people throughout their life. Many people don't believe they have a light to shine. They look about them and feel that somehow their talents don't measure up, aren't worthy, aren't needed. So they keep their light to themselves, truly believing that they have nothing to give. Yet Jesus tells each one of us, "You are the light of the world" (Matt. 5:14). Here Jesus is not speaking only to some who have been given special gifts or talents, but to everyone.

What can we do when "this little light of mine" seems shrouded in darkness? First of all, we can remember that the light was never ours to begin with, but God's. In John's Gospel, Jesus tells us, "I am the light of the world. Whoever follows me will never walk in darkness but will have the light of life" (John 8:12). Jesus is *the* light and can become *our* light when we acknowledge the One that dwells within each of us. The light that shines within us and outside us is the light of Christ given to us at baptism.

What has happened to the light given to you at baptism? Has it flourished and grown brighter over the years in service to Christ? Has it all but disappeared, because you've forgotten it's there? Or is it a combination of the two? Sometimes you're a huge beacon of light for all to see and at other times you can't decide what light you have or where it's supposed to shine? Or, has your light burned out?

To be beacons of light in a world filled with darkness, we need to nurture and focus on the light within us. This retreat gives all of us a wonderful opportunity to focus on the special gifts God has given to us and to each other. This weekend we are going to all help one another discover the many lights, the many gifts that each one of us has within us, just waiting to be uncovered. As we focus on that light and discover new ways to share it with others, we will come alive in Christ, not only as individuals, but also as a church.

To begin to look at the light given to us at baptism, it is helpful to discuss the meaning of this central act of the Christian faith. "Holy Baptism is full initiation by water and the Holy Spirit into Christ's Body, the Church. The bond which God establishes in Baptism is indissoluble."[1] So this covenant we have made with God is eternal. There's nothing we can do to get out of it. If we're baptized, we're baptized, and that's it. And in our baptism, we have all been made ministers. We're all ministers — and what is ministry? It's a whole new way of being, not just a way of doing.

To go into the ministry is not to be ordained, but to be baptized. Who are the ministers of your church? You are! Yes, you have clergy that serve your congregation, but you are the ministers. Throughout much of its history, the church has denied this scope of vocation to ministry and given higher credence and respect to clergy vocations. Today this church tradition is being guided back to an awareness of the breadth of vocation to ministry, notably in terms of its expression by the laity.

You all may have heard clergy saying that they want to "empower the laity." But of this concept, Stewart Zabriskie writes in his book *Total Ministry,* "I see this whole notion of 'empowering the laity' as being condescending to those who have been unable to do anything all along, which is far from the case. That same mind-set has also retranslated the word 'lay' to divert its roots in *laos* to a secondary and more popular sense of 'inexpert.' "[2] He goes on to say that an essential part of understanding the total ministry is to listen to those who are already ministering as Christ's body. "Listening is more important than devising systems to 'empower' the laity, those who are already expressing the Spirit's power."[3] Right now, I'd like us all to listen to ourselves and to each other.

3. (*Play appropriate music to help people get comfortable.*) Think back to a moment in your childhood when you felt really cared for, or when someone did something special for you. Name the person and what that person did; share it with your small group. (*The leader writes what each person says and then marks through the person's name and writes "Jesus," stating, "Jesus did this for you."*) Now, I want you to think of a time in your life when you did something for someone else. (*Write answers on newsprint.*) It's once again Jesus who did this for the other person, through you. You were sharing your gift of ministry with that other person.

4. Continue with large group discussion as follows:

In Colossians, St. Paul tells Archippus, "See that you fulfill the ministry which you have received in the Lord" (4:17, RSV). Each one of you here has already done that to some extent. And why? Because ministry takes place:

1. Wherever a Christian happens to be

2. Whenever a Christian is called to minister

3. With whomever a Christian happens to meet

4. Using whatever gifts a Christian has been given[4]

Before we leave, I'd like us to celebrate the light of Christ within each one of us, by taking a candle and lighting one another's candles, saying as we do so, "The light of Christ." Then when all of our candles are lit, we'll sing together, "This little light of mine, I'm going to let it shine, let it shine, let it shine."

5. At the end of this session, hand out "Scripture Passages about Community" (page 154). Ask each participant to select one passage to meditate on throughout the retreat, saying, "Keep the passage close to your heart. Let the words enter your very being. Bring this handout with you to the last session."

Session 2
Discerning Your Gifts

Materials Needed: Paper and thin marker for each participant, masking tape

Quotation: "Now there are varieties of gifts, but the same Spirit; and there are varieties of services, but the same Lord; and there are varieties of activities, but it is the same God who activates all of them in everyone." (1 Cor. 12:4–6)

1. Begin with the following talk or something similar:

In our last session, we talked about our vocation to ministry beginning with our baptism. Jesus' own baptism by John the Baptist in the Jordan River was the beginning of this new covenant between God and us. It was the beginning of Jesus' ministry, which continues through the covenant community. When you and I accept baptism, we become part of this ministry of Jesus. Paul told the Christians in Corinth, "Now you are the body of Christ and individually members of it" (1 Cor. 12:27).[5]

What does it mean to be part of the body of Christ? It means a lot of things. One of the most poignant passages of Scripture on this topic is when Paul tells us, "If one member suffers, all suffer together with it; if one member is honored, all rejoice together with it." (*Explain.*) It also means that we are all a different part of the same body. Read aloud 1 Corinthians 12:14–26. (*Explain.*)

Why is this such a difficult concept to grasp sometimes? Because we've all been shaped by Western individualism, which says I am my own person; I live for myself or my family alone; I rise and fall on my own merit. But Christianity is completely counter to this. Completely. If you don't take away anything from this retreat, please take away this. Being part of a Christian community means that we're never alone, or we don't have to be. We're all on a journey together. If one member suffers, everyone suffers with that person. If one member is honored, all rejoice. If we don't have a particular gift that is needed for ministry, someone else will. It means we're a *team* in the best sense of that word, not in competition for the best spot, because there is no best spot. All the spots are equal.

The former bishop of the Episcopal Diocese of Nevada tells the story of a Palm Sunday a number of years ago. His family had just come home directly from church, and he and his wife were in the kitchen preparing lunch. Suddenly their kindergartener came in from outside, stood in the doorway, and announced, "I can tell you what the people said when Jesus rode into town on a donkey." He paused, to make sure he had it just right and said, "Hosanna, I'm the highest."[6]

Let's sing that together, beginning as the little boy did and we'll add some more verses. Just repeat after me. "Hosanna, I'm the highest." (*Repeat*.) "Hosanna, I'm the lowest." (*Repeat*). "Hosanna, it doesn't matter." (*Repeat*).

And why not? Why doesn't it matter? (*Elicit responses from the group.*)

There does seem to be concern when we start talking about gifts for ministry, and this goes back to the time of St. Paul, about which gift is the best, who is the highest. This truly has nothing to do with what it means to be part of the body of Christ. Can we say that a hand is better than a foot, or a heart is better than a stomach? No, of course we can't. We have all been given the gifts of the Spirit at baptism, but there are varieties of gifts. An important question for every Christian is this: What particular gifts have been given to me through the Spirit and how can I use those gifts in the service of the Lord?

In 1 Corinthians, St. Paul tells us, "Now there are varieties of gifts, but the same Spirit; and there are varieties of services, but the same Lord; and there are varieties of activities, but it is the same God who activates all of them in everyone. To each is given the manifestation of the Spirit for the common good" (1 Cor. 12:4–7). He goes on to state that the gifts of the spirit are prophecy, administration, healing, preaching, discernment, and faith. The fruits of the spirit are love, joy, peace, patience, kindness, generosity, faithfulness, gentleness, and self-control (Gal. 5:22–23).

What are your gifts and fruits of the spirit? If you're like most people, you haven't really thought about it, or you may be certain that you have some gifts and not others. But there's only one way to test out what we think — and that's in community. So, here we are, all in community and we're going to see if how we perceive our gifts is the way others perceive them.

2. I want each of you to tape a piece of paper to your back and take a marker. You're then going to write on each other's papers, specifying the gifts that you perceive God has given to that person.

(*Everyone participates; then each reads his or her list of gifts.*) God has given and continues to give gifts to each person, and God does not want those gifts wasted. God's bounteous gifts stretch us as a community to find ways to use the gifts of each member in our mission. Paul was clear that the gifts were not given for individual use or glory, but rather for the common good. The shape of our mission, then, becomes reformed as each person with his or her unique gifts is incorporated into the Body. The metaphor of the gifted community takes us out of our individualism and challenges us to look at the implications of being a community created by God for God's purposes, as a gift to the world.[7]

3. Instruct participants to hold on to this list, as you will be using it in your next session. Between now and then ask them to think about one of their gifts they would like to write on their nametag to bring to the next session. Remind them also to bring the handout "Scripture Passages about Community" (page 154).

Session 3
Using Your Gifts in Community

Materials Needed: Meditation music, paper and pen for each participant, copies of "This Little Light of Mine"

Handout: "Scripture Passages about Community" (page 154)

Quotation: "To each is given the manifestation of the Spirit for the common good." (1 Cor. 12:7)

1. Play meditative music. Allow participants about one hour to meditate on their chosen Scripture passage and the gift they have chosen to put on their nametag. Instruct them as follows:

Repeat the Scripture text over and over, eventually zeroing in on a few words or even a single word. Keep repeating the words that you distilled from your text. Let God touch you through the word or words. Let these holy words take root in your being. Then add your gift. Listen to God's word for you. How do you feel God means for you to use your gift in community? If helpful, put your thoughts on the paper given to you. You'll have one hour for this exercise, so find a place where you can be comfortable.

2. Come back together in small groups. Have them share with one other person and then with the small group.

3. Gather the group together to share any insights they may have received during the retreat, to ask questions, or to make comments.

4. End by singing once again "This Little Light of Mine."

Chapter 12

Visioning Workshop

Additional
Leaders Needed: Facilitator for each table, two people to record answers on newsprint or PowerPoint

Materials Needed: Nametags, tape player and meditation music, two newsprint charts with markers or PowerPoint, microphone if group is large, paper and pen for each table facilitator, set of questions for each facilitator

Time Needed: Two hours

Handouts: Questions for small group discussion (page 155; for facilitators only)

Quotation: "Where there is no vision, the people perish." (Prov. 29:18, KJV)

Have meditation music playing as people arrive. It is preferable to have coffee and snacks available. Make sure everyone fills out a nametag. It is best to have people seated at tables of eight to ten, with one facilitator at each table. This allows large and small group discussion without people having to move.

1. When all are gathered, turn off the music. Welcome everyone warmly, introduce yourself, and give a brief overview of the exercise, as well as

---

This Visioning Workshop was planned by a committee chaired by the Rev. Canon Elizabeth Geitz and included Ms. Megan Callahan, the Rev. Virginia Hummel, Mr. Walter Marsden, and the Rev. Canon Juan Oliver. The Visioning Exercise is copyrighted by the Rev. Canon Juan Oliver, 1998, and is used here with permission.

the agenda for the day. Explain why your church is working on a mission strategy. Then state, "Before we can develop a strategy, we must listen to each other's dreams and visions for the future. Our program today is designed to help us do that. We'll begin with a visioning exercise in which I will take you through a series of visualizations designed to bring up the yearnings of your heart concerning the future of our worshiping community. Following that, we will have small group discussions about what you have just experienced. Then we'll meet again as a large group to put our collective vision together."

2. Establish the ground rules:

- Money is no object.

- Assume that your dreams can become a reality.

- Visualize your own congregation in the year 2025. By a miracle of modern medicine, you are the same age you are today.

- All visions are compatible. Please feel free to share your vision even if it seems to contradict someone else's. There is room for everyone's dreams.

3. Visioning Exercise (thirty minutes). Read the text slowly with pauses between each sentence. Where there is a series of dots, wait a few moments. Some people may want to write down their thoughts during the meditation, so it's best to give them that option.

Begin by taking some deep breaths. As you exhale, let the tension flow out of your body. It may be helpful to close your eyes. Relax. Get comfortable. Notice the feeling of your body against your chair. Notice the sounds in the room, the sounds outside. Become aware of your breathing.

Imagine yourself leaving your home on a Sunday morning. You go out the front door and walk across a field. At the far end of the field is a large building; maybe it's even a castle. You walk toward the building and see a long hall. Walk down it very slowly. . . . You see before you another door. Push open that door and walk out into a Sunday morning at some time in the future.

What are you wearing . . . ? Who else is going to church with you . . . ? How are you getting to church . . . ?

You see your church. As you're walking toward it, notice the changes in the building and in the surrounding area. Notice who else is approaching the building. How are they dressed...? What do they look like...? What are their ages, races, gender, ethnic origin...?

Approach the door and notice who greets you. Look at the bulletin and see how many services per weekend are offered. Walk into the church and prepare for the service. Notice how the service has changed...how the interior of the church has changed....

As the service proceeds, you come to the prayers for the people. The deacon, or lay leader, bids the people to pray for the needs of the surrounding community. Many people join in, praying aloud, concentrating on their ministries. Listen to the many kinds of ministries people are involved in. Where does ministry take place...? With whom does ministry take place...? Who are the ministers...?

As the service ends, you join others in a reception. There you meet a newcomer who has been attending for less than a month. You ask that person, "What do you like about this church...? What keeps you coming back...?" Listen to the answer.... Explain to the person that you used to be a member of this church many years ago and you're happy that new members are joining....

You then notice an old friend whom you haven't seen in twenty-five years. You're happy to see your friend and you ask, "Tell me. Why is there so much life here now...? What has happened over the last twenty-five years...?"

The person begins to explain to you, "Well, twenty-five years ago we made a decision to...." Listen to that decision.... Your friend explains how that decision has made a huge impact — bringing new life to the congregation, increasing membership, expanding ministry, ushering in a new chapter in the history of the church. You listen further as your friend explains how they had the courage to take such a bold step....

Gradually, you notice a feeling of well-being and satisfaction welling up inside you as you witness the new life that has come to the church you love so much. Finally, you say good-bye....

You walk out the door of the church, past the parking lot, across the field, toward the large building. Push open the door and walk slowly back down the long hall.... At the end, you find another door. Push it open and find yourself inside your home today.

As you feel comfortable, open your eyes. Look around you at your fellow travelers on this journey. Become conscious of the chair you're sitting in, your feet on the floor. Slowly, come back to this room in _____ [current year].

4. Small Group Discussion (twenty minutes). The table facilitator begins with a general question such as: "How did that feel for you?" then moves to the specific questions on the handout Questions for Small Group Discussion (page 155), related to different stages of the visioning exercise. The facilitator obtains everyone's response to each question before moving to the next, as a note taker writes down each response. When all answers have been gathered, the facilitator sums up that table's vision.

5. Large Group Discussion (thirty minutes). The visioning leader goes through the same set of questions, with the facilitators each responding for their table. At the end, the leader sums up the group's vision. Two people need to record alternating responses on the two newsprint charts at the front of the room or on PowerPoint. These lists will be turned over to the committee in charge of the visioning exercise. The results should then be reported to the congregation or judicatory as a whole.

When all responses have been gathered, the leader asks, "What prevents you from beginning to work toward achieving your vision today?" The leader then separates obstacles they can do something about from those they can't.

6. Discuss how wonderful it is that they've taken the time to participate in this program, how important it will be for the future, how you still need them to remain interested and involved, etc. Close with a prayer for the church, with participants adding their own petitions. (You might want to ask your table facilitators ahead of time to be prepared to offer a prayer.)

Chapter 13

Hospitality Evangelism Workshop

An imaginative, effective introduction of the hospitality evangelism program in your church is critical to promoting congregational ownership and involvement. Beginning with a sound theological basis for hospitality ministry, this workshop gives parishioners the biblical foundation for extending hospitality to the stranger along with the practical tools they will need to put that theology into practice.

In using this workshop it is best to follow some simple guidelines.

1. Ask participants to wear nametags during all sessions, to emphasize the importance of wearing them on Sunday mornings and at other church gatherings.

2. The quotation printed at the beginning of each session should be written on newsprint, or on a PowerPoint presentation, for all to see as they enter the room.

3. At the first session, give each participant a folder for handouts, as well as an agenda with dates filled in. At subsequent sessions, give out an agenda for that meeting along with the appropriate handouts.

This workshop can be used in several different formats. The first three sessions serve as excellent consciousness-raising material for the entire church. Every member of the church needs to be educated about hospitality ministry. Otherwise, the tendency is to assume that the hospitality committee is fulfilling this part of the church's responsibility. The importance of ownership of the program by everyone cannot be overstated. The last three sessions are designed for a smaller group of parishioners who are interested in developing a hospitality program for the church. In addition, Session 1 can be used to introduce the concept of hospitality to the poor.

Each session is designed to last sixty to ninety minutes and can be adapted to meet your particular needs.

If you do not already have in mind a lay chairperson or co-chairpersons to head your hospitality committee, note at the first two sessions anyone who seems to be taking a leadership role. This person may be a natural choice. It is important to have a chairperson in place by the end of Session 5, because she or he will lead Session 6.

AGENDA

Session 1 (Date: _____)
Fireweed Hospitality

Session 2 (Date: _____)
Christ in the Stranger's Guise

Session 3 (Date: _____)
"The Woman in the Purple Hat—
Why Do You Suppose She's in Church?"

Session 4 (Date: _____)
Components of Successful Hospitality Programs

Session 5 (Date: _____)
Components of Successful Hospitality Programs,
Continued—Where Do I Fit In?

Session 6 (Date: _____)
Putting It All Together

Session 1
Fireweed Hospitality

Materials Needed: Newsprint and marker or PowerPoint

Handouts: Workshop Agenda (above)

Quotation: "You know the heart of a stranger, for you were strangers in the land of Egypt." (Exod. 23:9, RSV)

1. Begin by reading the above quotation, in which God speaks to the Israelites on their exodus journey. Next, make the point that at some time in our lives each of us is the stranger; elaborate using the information found at the beginning of chapter 9 (pages 85ff.). Then ask, "When you were the stranger, what was in your heart? Who welcomed you and what did they do?" Give participants time to reflect on these questions; then ask each in turn to answer after giving his or her name.

2. Discuss the Judeo-Christian roots of hospitality, as described on pages 86–88.

3. Tell the story of the Whoopi Goldberg character in the movie *Sister Act,* as related on pages 88–89. Ask participants if they have ever felt like the Mother Superior. Have them share their thoughts with the person next to them.

4. Discuss the concept of Fireweed Hospitality, as presented on pages 88–92, and the radical hospitality extended by Jesus throughout his ministry. Stress that the distinctiveness of the Christian call to hospitality is in welcoming those who may be unwelcome in other settings. Ask participants for examples of when they have seen someone extend Fireweed Hospitality to someone else, or when they have done so themselves.

5. Discuss the Great Commandment (pages 59–66). What kinds of community outreach is your church involved in? What groups are not being helped? Explore the possibility of conducting a Community Needs Assessment, if desired (page 138).

Session 2
Christ in the Stranger's Guise

Materials Needed: Newsprint and marker or PowerPoint, a Bible, paper and pen for each participant

Handouts: "Rune of Hospitality" (page 146)

Christ Appearing as a Gardener to Mary Magdalene (page 147)

Quotation: "I was a stranger and you welcomed me." (Matt. 25:35)

1. Explore guest/host reversals in light of the discussion on pages 92–96, focusing on the stories of Sarah and Abraham and the three heavenly strangers, and Jesus and the strangers on the road to Emmaus.

2. Ask a participant to read aloud the "Rune of Hospitality" (page 146), and then give a copy to each participant, stressing the centrality of this message in the Christian call to welcome the stranger. Discuss the passage in the Gospel of John where Christ appears as a gardener to Mary Magdalene (page 147) and give each person the handout of Rembrandt's drawing. Then read aloud the quotation from Matthew 25:35 printed above.

3. How do we receive the Christ in the stranger's guise? First of all, by listening. Read aloud the following words from *The Listener*, by Taylor Caldwell:

> The most desperate need of people today is not . . . a new religion, or a new "way of life. . . . " People's real need, their most terrible need, is for someone to listen to them, not as a "patient," but as a human soul. They need to tell someone of what they think, of the bewilderment they encounter when they try to discover why they were born, how they must live, and where their destiny lies.[1]

Next, ask participants to think of a time in their lives when they felt they were really being listened to. What did the listener do? How did they feel when responded to in this way? Solicit answers from the group and write them on newsprint or PowerPoint.

4. To welcome others in the name of Christ, we need to be good story-listeners. As we listen to others, we need to engage in mutual listening for

the word of God revealed to us through the stranger. See pages 92–93 for more information on mutual listening.

5. As we become good story-listeners, we will at some point want to share our lives with those whom God sends our way. Help parishioners focus on what it means to "share the life" both as individuals and as a church. Begin by reading the following passage aloud:

> A faith-centered community, where the pastoral leadership is warm and caring, where the worship life offers quality extra-dependence, and people genuinely support and care for each other, offers something unavailable anywhere else. These churches have the gift of life, and they need to be taught to share this gift more freely with the seeking, hurting people who wander in their front door. Yet, often the members are so absorbed with drinking at and maintaining the fountain, that they fail to move over so that others can have some of this life-giving water.[2]

What we as a church have to share is this gift of life that has been freely given to each one of us by God — and to each and every person who cares enough to take the time to walk in our door and sit in our pew. Newcomer programs at their heart are about sharing this life, this community, your life, your community.

6. How can a congregation successfully "share the life"? On two levels, both individually and corporately. Individually, we are each unique and God has given each one of us gifts to share. Read 1 Corinthians 12:4– 11 aloud. Encourage participants to reflect on the gifts God has given them that they might share with others. If participants are unclear about their particular gifts you may want to offer the Gift Discernment Retreat (pages 110–116). It is best not to explore their individual gifts within this workshop setting since it is a time-consuming process that can divert energy from your primary focus.

Corporately, your parish has much to share with the newcomer. Give each participant a piece of paper and a pen. Ask group members to reflect for a minute on what it is they like about your church. Have them write down what they believe the strengths of your parish are now, and then what they could be in the future. Invite each participant to read her or his list aloud. Write the group's comments on newsprint or PowerPoint. At the next session, provide a photocopy for each participant.

Session 3
"The Woman in the Purple Hat—
Why Do You Suppose She's in Church?"

Materials Needed: Newsprint and marker or PowerPoint

Handouts: Photocopies of the list of congregational strengths developed in Session 2

Newcomer Scenarios (page 148)

Hello, I Am a Newcomer to Your Church (page 149)

Quotation: "Contribute to the needs of the saints; extend hospitality to strangers." (Rom. 12:13)

1. Begin by distributing the list of strengths composed by participants at the last gathering. Read several aloud as you remind them that they have a great deal to share as a congregation.

2. Read the quotation aloud. State that today's session will focus on the variety of needs that bring newcomers to church.

The woman in the purple hat — why do you suppose she's in church?[3] This question is a good one to raise when developing a hospitality program. Why have new people decided to worship here? What do they seek? Give out your own version of Newcomer Scenarios, or use the handout on page 148. Have different parishioners read them aloud one at a time. After each, discuss the needs of the newcomer described.

3. Ask participants to reflect for a moment on what they seek from the church. Why do they set their alarms on Sunday morning for church rather than sleeping late or reading the Sunday paper? Have participants share their reflections in groups of two for five minutes. Then present the findings to the group as a whole. Write these reflections on newsprint or PowerPoint.

4. It is helpful to tell participants that newcomers' reasons for seeking the church are often similar to their own. Research has shown that people most often seek the church for (a) refreshment, support, growth, fulfillment, faith, and fellowship; (b) their family, help in raising children,

keeping relationships together; and (c) for a sense of belonging. In addition, many reported a significant change in their lives that preceded their reinvolvement with church life. Generally, people do not seek the church during a crisis. Instead, their reinvolvement is connected with the restructuring and reordering of their lives after the crisis.[4] State that everyone experiences the universal life events of birth, death, illness, and, possibly moving, changing jobs, or new responsibilities at work. Such life experiences, common to us all, may bring a person to seek the church.[5] Thus, each participant will have unique gifts to share with the newcomer — gifts that no one else can or will share in quite the same way.

5. To close this session, distribute the handout Hello, I Am a Newcomer to Your Church (page 149). Ask one of them to read it aloud to the group. (This is also an excellent reflective piece to print in your church newsletter as you introduce your hospitality evangelism program to the congregation at large.)

Session 4
Components of Successful Hospitality Programs

Materials Needed: Newsprint and markers or PowerPoint

Handouts: Welcome Brochure (pages 139–140)

                          Act of Friendship Tablet (page 141)

                          Welcoming Letter (page 142)

                          Newcomer History (page 150)

Quotation: "Enlarge the site of your tent, and let the curtains of your habitations be stretched out; do not hold back; lengthen your cords and strengthen your stakes." (Isa. 54:2)

1. Begin by saying that to "enlarge the site of our tents" and to "stretch out our curtains" today requires a comprehensive hospitality program for attracting, inviting, greeting, calling, orienting, and incorporating new members. In establishing such a program, it is important to state at the

outset that the goal of hospitality programs is for newcomers to become Christ's conscious agents in their daily lives — at work, at home, in the community, in the area of citizenship, in leisure activities, as well as within the church. Without this vision for mission in the world, a church's hospitality program can be centered inward toward the needs of the individual congregation, rather than outward toward the needs of the world. This outward vision is foundational to a sound hospitality program and should be articulated throughout the remaining workshop sessions.

Next, participants should be urged to begin thinking about which part of the program they might want to work on further. *After each of the following sections, have them brainstorm ways they might implement that segment of the program in their church.* Write their ideas on newsprint and save it. In this introductory workshop, it is helpful to give participants more ideas than they can use. This gives them the freedom to put together their own program, which will promote group ownership of the project.

2. Present the information below in lecture format, along with the information on pages 71–72.

a. Lutheran Church historian Martin Marty says that one word defines the difference between churches that grow and those that don't: *invite*. Marty reports a study that indicates that the average Episcopalian invites someone to church once every twenty-eight years. His statistic may be an exaggeration, but his point is not. When a church isn't growing, its members are not "inviting."[6]

Research has shown that three out of four people who were not previously attending church were influenced by a friend or family member to come to church. The body of Christ grows person-by-person, family-by-family, through a layperson who cares enough about a friend, neighbor, colleague, or family member to offer her or him a bridge to relationship with Christ and his church. If the invitation does not begin with loving concern, it will not succeed.[7]

One way to encourage inviting is by scheduling an Invite-a-Friend or Bring-a-Friend Sunday in your church. This method has been used by hundreds of congregations during the last five years. A pastor in Mulvane, Kansas, says, "In five years, we have had a total of 275 visitors to worship at our five Bring-a-Friend Sundays. Many of these persons subsequently joined our church."[8] It is important to stress that the invitation is always God's, not ours nor our church's.[9] Invitations should be extended only after prayerful consideration by the person doing the inviting.

A fast-growing United Methodist church in Richland, Washington, has used the following method twice a year for several years. A few weeks before Christmas and Easter, the pastor schedules five minutes of meditative background music in the morning worship service. After the ushers distribute three-by-five-inch cards, the pastor asks worshipers to write down the names of everyone they can think of who does not attend church. He then asks them to pray for those people every day for the next two weeks. During morning worship two weeks later, he urges worshipers to invite to church those people for whom they have been praying. Average worship attendance has grown from three hundred to twelve hundred during the past dozen years.[10]

b. To attract other people to your congregation, intentional outreach to those who do not presently attend church is key. To begin a program of this nature, focused on the Great Commission to "Go into all the world and proclaim the good news to the whole creation" (Mark 16:15), think carefully about who the people are in your area who may be seeking a church home. The question is not, "What do *you* like?" but "What would *they* like?" To compile a profile of the average person in your community who does not attend church, ask yourself these questions. Are they primarily disaffected Roman Catholics? Former Southern Baptists? Pentecostals? Have they or their parents never attended a church?

An adult forum with small groups in which the following questions are addressed can be helpful in developing this program:

1. What does the average person in our community, who does not attend church, think of "church" generally?

2. What might motivate this person to come to church?

3. What are the two or three characteristics about our church that would be most attractive to them?

In addition, you might look at the demographics of your community as well as the life issues of the people within it. Keep in mind that 80 percent of the decisions about going to church are made by women. Thus, consideration of the issues that concern women is critical.

Taking out a good-sized ad in the Yellow Pages is money well spent. This is the first place most newcomers in a community look when searching for a church home. It is worth paying extra for a large ad that gets your unique message across. Be sure to include your telephone number in large letters, a map, an e-mail address, and a website location. The advertisement will more than pay for itself.

c. Contacting people who have recently moved into your area is another way to reach out beyond the walls of your church. Since people new to your community are in transition, they are often receptive to a church's welcoming invitation. Churches that want to follow this route will want to keep in mind that people expect professionally printed material today. A color postcard with a catchy phrase on the front is best. *A minimum of three cards need to be mailed to achieve a positive result.* The most cost-effective way to obtain these cards is by ordering them through a company that mass produces them. See Cokesbury.com, keyword postcard.

d. Using printed material to "advertise" can reach large numbers of people with minimal expense. Articles about church activities can be sent to local newspapers along with pictures. This is usually free and reaches a large number of people. In some churches a community newsletter has been an effective way to reach people who live near the church. The emphasis here is on your congregation's role as neighbor. Offerings at the church that might be of interest in the community should also be highlighted, such as church school and adult education events, guest speakers, discovery or seeker classes, Bible study, and concerts.[11] In addition, a well-publicized, well-run vacation church school can provide outreach to young families.

Paid-for advertisements are also worthwhile. The Church Ad Project offers numerous catchy advertisements suitable for the newspaper. One year at Christmastime my church ran an ad with the title, "Whose Birthday Is It Anyway?" with a picture of Santa Claus on one side and Jesus on the other. We received a number of thank-you letters from people in the community, most of whom were not members of our church. To obtain the Church Ad Project catalogue call 800-331-9391, or see www.churchad.com.

e. Reflecting on the appearance of the church facility can help parishioners see their church in a new light. Instruct participants to shut their eyes and picture themselves approaching their church with no previous knowledge of it. What do they see? Are there signs out front that are clearly visible from the road? What is the general condition of the church? Does it look inviting, welcoming? If not, what can easily be changed?

Next, have them imagine what it would be like to walk into the church building for the first time. Are areas clearly marked with attractive, permanent signs? For example, would guests know where to find the nursery, church school, parish hall, rest rooms, church offices? Is the interior of the church well maintained? Do the walls need a new coat of paint? Do the floors need to be professionally waxed? *First impressions count.* We tell our guests much about our church by both interior and exterior appearances.

f. Is there a tract rack in your church? If not, discuss the possibility of obtaining one. If there is a tract rack, discuss its location. Is it visible to everyone who comes into your church? Is there a rack in more than one location? Does it contain information about Christianity for seekers who may not ever have attended church? How about your denomination and your particular congregation? Your Welcome Brochure (pages 139–140) should be prominently displayed here as well.

4. a. One concern shared by many parishioners as they consider extending hospitality to the stranger might be discussed in terms of balance. Whereas parishioners should not ignore new people, neither should they bombard them with greetings.

Another frequent concern of parishioners when making an effort to welcome newcomers is that the person they believe is a newcomer may actually be a member of long-standing. The awkwardness of this situation can be prevented by simply saying to the person, "I don't believe I've met you. I'm _____." Regardless of how long a person may have been attending the church, if he or she is new to you, you should make an effort to meet that person.

b. Discuss the role of hospitality ministers as greeters on Sunday morning, as discussed on page 99.

c. Distribute the handouts Act of Friendship Tablet (page 141),[12] Welcoming Letter (page 142), and Newcomer History (page 150). Discuss their use in light of the material on pages 101–105.

d. Discuss the use of nametags during adult education events and coffee hour (hospitality hour) as related on page 101.

Session 5
Components of Hospitality Programs, Continued —
Where Do I Fit In?

Materials Needed: Newsprint and markers or PowerPoint

Handouts: Newcomer Forum Invitation (page 151)

Newcomer News (page 151)

Introduction to Covenant Groups (page 152)

Request for Letter of Transfer (page 153)

New Member Dedication Litany (page 145)

Quotation: "Let mutual love continue. Do not neglect to show hospitality to strangers, for by doing that some have entertained angels without knowing it." (Heb. 13:1–2)

1. Begin by reading aloud the following story from Herb Miller's *How to Build a Magnetic Church:*

> The pastor was astonished at his welcome. He had just arrived at an ancient Coptic monastery out in the desert, nearly a day's journey from Cairo, Egypt. The monks treated him as if he were the one important guest they had been awaiting since the place was established in the twelfth century. They served a fine meal, showed him to a comfortable room, and brought him

a bouquet of flowers. He was then greeted by the abbot of the monastery, Father Jeremiah.

"Wow!" said the pastor. "You sure know how to treat visitors."

Father Jeremiah replied, "We always treat guests as if they were angels, just to be safe."[13]

State that this Coptic monastery had put into practice the words from Hebrews in today's quotation; then read the quotation aloud. Comment on the number of angels in their community who may be unknown to participants at this time — angels who are waiting to be welcomed and visited by them.

3. a. The lay calling system enables us to visit God's many angels and is the cornerstone of any hospitality program. First, discuss the concept of hospitality ministers as both Sunday morning greeters and Sunday afternoon callers. See pages 101–105 for details of this program. Be sure to stress the research findings on calling the day of a person's first visit, and on lay calls versus clergy calls for the initial visit.

b. After describing the program, ask participants how they would feel about making a call. Address any concerns they may have.

4. Orienting both newcomers and parishioners is the first step in the important process of integration. New members can be educated by covenant groups, a newcomer forum, and a newcomer party, as well as through contact with their "shepherds" and other parishioners. Distribute copies of the Newcomer Forum Invitation (page 151), discussing the type of newcomer party and forum your church might host. The invitation can be a simple postcard giving the necessary information. It should be signed by the person leading the forum. Your newcomer party invitation should be designed by you to fit the party planned. Both invitations should be mailed three to four weeks before the event. Be sure also to include several announcements in your church newsletter and Sunday leaflet.

The congregation is educated through churchwide newcomer events, rotation of coffee hour greeters and nametag table hosts, and Newcomer News. Discuss the sample Newcomer News (page 151).

A bulletin board in the church hall can serve as a pictorial directory for parishioners and newcomers alike. Snapshots, regularly updated, of older and newer members with their names posted below can be fun for everyone as well as helpful. Pictures of various church groups can serve as an additional guide for new people.

5. Discuss the New Member Dedication Litany described on page 106 and hand out a copy of the Litany (page 145).

6. Integration into the congregation can be one of the most difficult stages for newcomers. Once the initial welcomes are over, there needs to be a structured system in place to enable newcomers to come to-gether and know each other in a more intimate environment. For this purpose, the covenant group program is superb. Tell about this new member incorporation program, discussed on page 107, and hand out copies of Introduction to Covenant Groups (page 152) and Request for Letter of Transfer (page 153). In addition, tell about the Guild of the Christ Child, using baptismal sponsors, described on page 106–7.

At the end of this session, ask each person to sign up for the part of the program she or he wishes to work on further. Write group members' selections on newsprint or PowerPoint. Participants should be prepared to make recommendations to the group in two weeks on the portions of the program they have chosen to use. As participants leave, give them the newsprint or PowerPoint handout with brainstorming ideas for their particular sections.

Session 6
Putting It All Together

Materials Needed: Newsprint and markers or PowerPoint

Handouts: None

Quotation: "Listen! I am standing at the door, knocking; if you hear my voice and open the door, I will come in to you and eat with you, and you with me." (Rev. 3:20)

1. Begin by reading the quotation aloud. Talk of the excitement of finally getting to the point of putting your own evangelism/hospitality program

together, stressing the many gifts and surprises that await those who welcome the Christ in the stranger's guise.

2. Discuss and decide how the overall program will be structured and implemented. Go around the room and have participants share what they have decided with the group. The new hospitality chairperson should lead this session. The hospitality committee should decide upon the number and date of future gatherings.

After this session, type each section heading with the name of the person responsible for it, along with the ideas that will be put into effect. Mail it to participants along with the biggest thank-you imaginable for their time and effort!

Appendix

Handouts and Forms

As lay leaders begin to assume the authority that is theirs, they will need concrete tools for implementing and running lay ministry programs in their church. Establishing a successful newcomer program takes not only the knowledge of what should be included, but numerous forms to put the program into effect. Since their development can be time-consuming, forms are provided here that have been used to implement the programs described.

Most of the forms are generic. Therefore, they can be typed or photocopied onto your own letterhead and used as is. However, you may want to personalize them to reflect your particular church.

COMMUNITY NEEDS ASSESSMENT INTERVIEW FORM

Date _____

Interview with _____

Organization _____

Address _____

Telephone _____ E-mail _____

1. How does the social service network in _____ handle emergencies?

2. Who asks you for help? How do you handle it?

3. What needs, normally met through social service agencies, are not currently being met here?

4. Do you know why the social service sector is not meeting these needs?

5. Are there any plans under way to establish an agency to meet these needs?

6. If a new ministry was established, what range of services would you like to see it provide?

7. What are the funding sources in this community for establishing such an outreach?

8. Who currently administers emergency funds in this community?

9. How are utility funds administered?

10. Ideally, how would you see area churches, synagogues, and other religious organizations participating in this venture?

11. What do you see as potential problem areas that might arise in (a) establishing this ministry, (b) running it?

12. Any other comments?

13. Who else do you recommend we interview?

Elizabeth R. Geitz, *On Loving Our Neighbors*
(Plainfield, N.J.: Wardens and Vestry of Grace Church, 1988), 14.

[See pages 64–65 and 123]

WELCOME BROCHURE

The following was used in a welcome brochure prepared for Trinity Church, Princeton, New Jersey, an Episcopal congregation in the Diocese of New Jersey. The presentation was enhanced by appropriate graphic elements and photos depicting parish life. Here we provide only the text.

The people and clergy of Trinity Church welcome you into our community. We hope you will find spiritual nourishment and companionship with us as you seek a new church home.

Trinity Church, Princeton, is an Episcopal church in the American branch of the worldwide Anglican Communion. We have deep historic roots and also a willingness to open ourselves to the issues of the contemporary world.

As Episcopalians we look to scripture, tradition, reason, and experience as authority for our faith and worship. These provide a framework for understanding ourselves and our salvation and the way we are meant to live in relationship to God and one another. Our life of worship is centered in the Holy Eucharist, and we encourage you to join us in receiving communion.

In addition to Sunday morning worship and Adult Education Forums, there are smaller weekday services, coffee and fellowship times, study and prayer groups, choirs, and active Church School and Youth Fellowship programs. As prayer and reflection lead us to action, there are many opportunities for service to those within the parish and beyond who are in need of help.

We hope that the moment will come when you will want to become a member of Trinity, to move beyond companionship to commitment. What follows in this pamphlet is intended to help you do that. In the meantime, we encourage you to enter into our life as fully as you can. If you have filled out the Act of Friendship Tablet, our newcomer liaison will be in touch with you soon. We are all on a journey of faith, and we welcome you, whatever your convictions, doubts, and hopes.

Becoming a Member

As Christians we are always growing in faith. You may be someone who...

- has never attended church and wants to learn about the Christian faith.
- seeks baptism.

- is not an Episcopalian and desires Confirmation or to be received into the Episcopal Church.
- is new in the community and wishes to transfer membership.
- has a child in our Church School or choir and who wishes to know more about our liturgy and Prayer Book.
- is a member of long-standing in the Episcopal Church who seeks to refresh your knowledge.

We want you to become a member. When you are ready to take that step, make an appointment with one of the clergy to discuss your particular concern. The clergy look forward to meeting with you and becoming better acquainted.

Membership classes at Trinity are for newcomers, but also for those who are not new in our midst but may want more adult education about being an Episcopalian. "The Episcopal Church: A Personal Investigation" is the name of our series of classes taught by clergy and laity. These classes give an Anglican perspective on the meaning of our Baptismal vows, Confirmation commitment, and our continual reaffirmation of faith.

As a Member We Ask You . . .

- to be faithful in Sunday worship, realizing that celebrating the Eucharist together is essential to our life as the Body of Christ.
- to be dedicated in service, supporting with time and effort the ministries of Trinity. Here is one of the important ways we gain our personal experience of God; through service we meet Christ in others.
- to be responsible in pledging, conscientious in financial support of the church. This gives meaning to our prayer in the Eucharist that we "may honor you with our substance and be faithful stewards of your bounty."

Trinity Parish was founded in 1833. In the colonial period, it was a preaching station of the Trenton mission. The current church, built in 1868, was designed by Richard Upjohn, who designed Trinity, Wall Street, New York, and other historic buildings in the Gothic Revival style. The church on Mercer Street was modified by the architect Ralph Adams Cram, designer of the Princeton University Chapel. The gallery organ was built on classic French design principles by Casavant Frères, Limitée, Quebec, in 1978.

We want you to feel at home with us, and we hope you have a sense of expectancy and joy as you join our community at Trinity.

[See pages 104, 127, and 131]

ACT OF FRIENDSHIP TABLET

Date: _____

call from Chad's?

"You shall love the Lord your God with all your heart . . . And your neighbor as yourself" (Luke 10:27). These words of Jesus Christ are the setting for our worship, but sometimes we forget to love those who worship with us. Take time to get to know the people beside you; sign this tablet and pass it to others in your pew.

Worshiper (Regular members need only give their names and check "member.")	Member	Guest	New Resident	Other	Desire Membership Information	Telephone
Name (Ms., Mrs., Mr.)						Home
Address, Zip						Work
Name (Ms., Mrs., Mr.)						Home
Address, Zip						Work
Name (Ms., Mrs., Mr.)						Home
Address, Zip						Work
Name (Ms., Mrs., Mr.)						Home
Address, Zip						Work
Name (Ms., Mrs., Mr.)						Home
Address, Zip						Work
Name (Ms., Mrs., Mr.)						Home
Address, Zip						Work
Name (Ms., Mrs., Mr.)						Home
Address, Zip						Work

[See pages 101-102, 127, and 132]

WELCOMING LETTER

Dear _____

We are pleased you have begun to worship with us and hope that in your time here you have experienced some of the joy of God's love that brings us together each week.

The enclosed brochure will give you a sense of our life as a Christian community. In addition, in the entrance to the church you will find the latest copy of our church news bulletin. It will inform you of our current programs and activities; we sincerely hope you will feel free to participate in those that interest you.

In order to assist you further, it would be helpful if you could complete the enclosed form and return it to us in the self-addressed envelope. The more we know your needs, the better we will be able to meet them.

We are delighted you are worshiping with us and look forward to getting to know you. If you would like more information about our church or if there are any pastoral needs in which I can assist you, please call me.

[See pages 104, 127, and 132]

NEWCOMER INFORMATION SHEET

Name(s) _____ Date _____

Address _____

_____

Phone _____ E-mail _____

Time of Church Service Usually Attended _____

LIST THE NAME AND DATE OF BIRTH FOR EACH FAMILY MEMBER.
IF YOU HAVE CHILDREN, PLEASE LIST SCHOOL OR COLLEGE
AND CURRENT GRADE LEVEL.

I WOULD LIKE INFORMATION ABOUT:

___ Acolytes   ___ Outreach Programs
___ Altar Guild   ___ Pastoral Services
___ Baptism   ___ Retreats
___ Choirs   ___ Women's Group
___ Church School   ___ Youth Group
___ Confirmation

NEWCOMER INFORMATION SHEET

(continued)

IN THIS SPACE, PLEASE GIVE US ANY OTHER INFORMATION
YOU WOULD LIKE OUR CLERGY TO KNOW.

FOR OFFICE USE ONLY

[See page 104]

NEW MEMBER DEDICATION LITANY

Welcoming
Committee: I/We present _____ who have de-
cided to become members of _____
Church.

Celebrant: Do you believe God has led you to _____
Church as your spiritual home?

Candidates: *I do.*

Celebrant: Will you faithfully support the worship and the ministries of
_____ Church with your prayers and
participation?

Candidates: *I will, with God's help.*

Celebrant: Will you continue to follow Jesus Christ by loving the Lord
your God with all your heart and your neighbor as yourself?

Candidates: *I will, with God's help.*

Celebrant: As you have been led here, will you seek to lead others to
Christ and to the church?

Candidates: *I will, with God's help.*

Celebrant: In the name of God and of this congregation, we welcome
you to _____ Church.

Congregation: *We welcome you into the Body of Christ known as _____
_____ Church and look forward to continuing to
grow in fellowship with you.*

Celebrant: Please join us in the sharing of the peace, a symbol of our
greeting and our joy: The peace of the Lord be always
with you.

Congregation: *And also with you.*

Written by the Rev. Christopher Brdlik and the Rev. Canon Elizabeth R. Geitz
for Calvary Episcopal Church, Summit, New Jersey, and used with permission.

[See pages 106, 132, and 134]

Rune of hospitality

i saw a stranger yestreen;
i put food in the eating place,
drink in the drinking place,
music in the listening place;
and in the blessed name of the triune
he blessed myself and my house,
my cattle and my dear ones.
   and the lark said in her song
      often, often, often,
         goes the christ in the stranger's guise;
      often, often, often,
goes the christ in the stranger's guise.

[See pages 94 and 124]

Christ Appearing as a Gardener to Mary Magdalene.
Rembrandt. Circa 1643. Amsterdam

[See pages 94 and 124]

NEWCOMER SCENARIOS

1. I've just moved here with my husband and new baby. I started a part-time job last week to help out with our bills. With a new baby, a new job, and a new community to get acquainted with, I feel pulled in several directions at once. I've been to your church four times.

2. I'm single and I live a thousand miles from my parents, brothers, and sisters. I have no family nearby so I'm looking for a church family. My job is taking up more and more of my time, and I'm finding it difficult to have much of a social life. I moved here two years ago but just began seeking a church home last month.

3. I stopped going to church for a while, but I just feel that I want to come back right now. I feel peaceful here, even though it's different from my former church home. It's strange, yet somehow familiar to me. I don't want to join a committee now. I've done all of that. I just want to feel the peace of the worship services. My mother died last year and I feel better after church—closer to God and, I guess, to my mother in some way.

4. I left the institutional church ten years ago over the issue of inclusive language. I didn't think I could hear "Father, Son, and Holy Spirit" one more time. I learned in my college religion class that God is neither Father or Mother, that God is both/and, but the church seems unaware of this. I heard through a friend that there's a great Women's Spirituality Group here so I thought I'd give it one more try.

5. I have been homeless for four years now and spend most of my time on the streets. It's not a bad way of life, really. I've gotten used to it. The only way I can survive, though, is through my faith. I was walking past this church one Sunday and heard the music. It sounded so beautiful; I decided to come in. I know I don't exactly dress like everyone else, but it's important for me to be here. This place feels like home to me.

[See page 126]

HELLO, I AM A NEWCOMER TO YOUR CHURCH

You cannot know the reason why I am here this morning. It may be as simple as a move to your community or as complicated as personal crisis that leads me to seek strength from God. In either case, I am here. And I will probably remain here and come back to worship with you next Sunday and the Sunday after and the Sunday after that, if you will do some things for me. Won't you please...

- Smile at me as I walk in the door. You are my first impression of the church during the first few moments I am in your building, and this first impression will probably stay with me a long time.

- Help me find my place in the service. I will not find your help an intrusion. In fact, I will remember your kindness.

- Speak to me during the coffee hour. I know you want to see your friends and settle that piece of committee business. But I may find it hard to believe that you truly care for each other unless I first see evidence that you care for "the stranger in your midst."

- Tell me good things about your church and your minister. I want to believe that I have come to a place where people love each other and where they believe that they are doing something exciting and important for the Lord.

- Notice me — even if I am not a "family." I don't want to feel invisible just because I am unmarried, a single parent, a teenager, or an older person.

- Talk to me again the second week when I come back, and the third and the fourth. I am still not a part of your parish family. Please don't feel you have "done your duty" by me just because you made a point of greeting me the first week I was here.

- Invite me to become part of some church group or organization. I need more than worship every Sunday. I need to know that I am accepted and affirmed by a group of people within the church who know me by my first name and who care about me as an individual.

If you can find it in your heart to do these things for me, I will come back... the second Sunday, the third, and maybe forever. I will worship with you, and I may join your choir, work at your fair, teach in your church school, contribute to your canvas, and become a highly involved member of your church, and, in so doing, I will find my own life immeasurably enriched.

Written by the Rev. Christopher Chamberlin Moore and used with permission.

[See pages 126 and 127]

NEWCOMER HISTORY

Name _____

Address _____

City, State, Zip _____

Phone _____ E-mail _____

Comments:

1. First visit   _____

2. Hospitality minister   _____

3. Second visit   _____

4. Third visit   _____

5. Letter and information sheet sent   _____

6. Information sheet returned and given
    to clergy for follow-up   _____

7. Shepherd assigned   _____

8. Further visits   _____

9. Covenant program information sent   _____

10. Date of one-year anniversary visit made   _____

[See pages 103–4, 127, and 132]

NEWCOMER FORUM INVITATION

All newcomers are invited to a special Newcomer Forum on _____ at _____. Our Christian education, youth, worship and music programs, and pastoral and outreach ministries will be discussed.

Please join us for a brief presentation, a question-and-answer period, and fellowship. I hope to see you there!

[See pages 132 and 133]

NEWCOMER NEWS

Several parishioners have recently volunteered their services to our Newcomer Program. _____ and _____ will be co-chairing the nametag table during forum time; _____ will be working on the newcomer party. Please call any of us with your ideas, suggestions, or comments. In addition, _____ parishioners made newcomer calls last year!

Welcoming new people is a responsibility we all share. Please look out for the many new people who will be joining us over the summer. Since most activities break during July and August, this is an especially difficult time for new people. We welcome the following people into the life of our church family.

(*After obtaining permission,* the newcomer's name, the names and ages of children [if any], address, and telephone number can be listed here.)

[See pages 106, 132, and 133]

INTRODUCTION TO COVENANT GROUPS

Christianity is relentlessly corporate. That means that God calls individuals to-gether in the church to discover their unity of spirit in spite of their diversity. This is the way Jesus worked with his disciples. People with differing gifts, personal-ities, backgrounds, and needs are all brought together in the body of Christ. It is a continuing miracle.

The small groups in our covenant program are not just discussion groups; they are little churches-in-formation. You will share your insights and experiences in order that to some degree you may be obedient to Jesus' command: "Bear one another's burdens." In your groups you are not just talking about the church, you are being the church; not just talking about Christ, but becoming the body of Christ.

Each covenant group has a convener, a member of our church who will be your companion during the course of the program. He or she is not a teacher or leader, but a growing Christian like you whose job it is to help your group accomplish its tasks while sharing fully with you in your journey.

Prayer will be part of your group's experience: brief, simple, spontaneous, and honest. Christian communities live on prayer as surely as they live on the air they breathe. Please enter into your group experience trusting the Spirit of God to guide you, trusting the Spirit of God who is "the Lord and Giver of Life" in the church.

Your faithful attendance is essential. Your group's experience will be diminished by any absences. But if you are sick and cannot attend, please call your leader so your group can keep you in its prayers.

God bless you on your journey.

Developed by All Saints Church, Pasadena, California, and used with permission.

[See pages 107, 132, and 134]

REQUEST FOR LETTER OF TRANSFER

To the Rector or Minister in charge of _____

Address: _____

_____

This is to request a Letter of Transfer for:

_____

      Children (if applicable): _____

      _____

      _____

      _____

(It would be appreciated if you would include pertinent dates, i.e., Birth, Baptism, Confirmation.)

Thank you.

      Signed: _____

      Address: _____

      _____

Please mail the completed Letter of Transfer directly to the church from which the request is being made. It should be returned to our church office at the above address.

[See pages 132 and 134]

SCRIPTURE PASSAGES ABOUT COMMUNITY

1. I, Yahweh, speak with directness. I express myself with clarity. Assemble, come, gather together...consult with each other (Isa. 45:19, 20, 21, JB).

2. Where two or three are gathered in my name, there am I in the midst of them (Matt. 18:20, RSV).

3. The saints together make a unity in the work of service, building up the body of Christ (Eph. 4:12, JB).

4. Let us consider how to stir up one another to love and good works, not neglecting to meet together...but encouraging one another (Heb. 10:24-25, RSV).

5. If one member [of the Body of Christ] suffers, all suffer together with it; if one member is honored, all rejoice together with it (1 Cor. 12:26, NRSV).

6. Now the whole group of those who believed were of one heart and soul (Acts 4:32, NRSV).

7. Moses' father-in-law said to him, "What you are doing is not good. You will surely wear yourself out, both you and these people with you. For the task is too heavy for you; you cannot do it alone" (Exod. 18:17-18, NRSV).

8. The whole body is fitted and joined together, every joint adding its own strength (Eph. 4:16, JB).

9. They called the church together and related all that God had done with them (Acts 14:27, NRSV).

10. Now there are varieties of gifts, but the same Spirit....To each is given the manifestation of the Spirit for the common good (1 Cor. 12:4, 7, NRSV).

[See pages 110, 112, and 115]

QUESTIONS FOR SMALL GROUP DISCUSSION

1. What were you wearing on the way to church? Who else was with you? How did you get there?

2. What changes did you notice in the church building and surrounding area?

3. Who else was walking into church? How were they dressed? What did they look like?

4. What was their age, race, gender, ethnic origin?

5. Who greeted you at the door?

6. How many services were there per week? How had the service changed?

7. How had the interior of the church changed?

8. What ministries did the people pray about? Where did they take place? Who were the ministers?

9. What did the newcomer tell you that she or he liked about the church?

10. How did your old friend respond when you asked what had happened to bring such new life into the church?

11. How did the congregation have the courage to take such a bold step?

[See pages 117 and 120]

Notes

Chapter 1: Seeing the Elephant

1. Marcus Borg, *The Heart of Christianity: Rediscovering a Life of Faith* (San Francisco: HarperSanFrancisco, 2003), 3, 20.

2. W. Paul Jones, *Theological Worlds: Understanding the Alternative Rhythms of Christian Belief* (Nashville: Abingdon Press, 1989), 12, 16.

3. Richard Stoll Armstrong, "Evangelism," in *The Westminster Dictionary of Christian Theology*, ed. Alan Richardson and John S. Bowden (Philadelphia: Westminster Press, 1983), 193.

4. Quoted in Borg, *The Heart of Christianity*, 208–9.

Chapter 2: Blazing a New Path

1. Raimundo Panikkar, "The Jordan, the Tiber, and the Ganges," in *The Myth of Christian Uniqueness: Toward a Pluralistic Theology of Religions*, ed. John Hick and Paul Knitter (Maryknoll, N.Y.: Orbis Books, 1987), 93–95. In the preface, Knitter writes: "We are calling 'Christian uniqueness' a 'myth' not because we think that talk of the uniqueness of Christianity is purely and simply false.... Rather we feel that such talk, like all mythic language, must be understood carefully; its 'truth' lies not on its literal surface but within its ever-changing historical and personal meaning. This book, then, rather than intending to deny Christian uniqueness, wants to interpret it anew."

2. Bernard Lewis, *What Went Wrong? Western Impact and Middle Eastern Response* (New York: Oxford University Press, 2002), 4.

3. Quoted in John Hick, *God Has Many Names* (Philadelphia: Westminster Press, 1980), 27.

4. Karl Barth, *Church Dogmatics* I/2, 357, as quoted in Hick, *God Has Many Names*, 8.

5. John Hick, "The Non-Absoluteness of Christianity," in *The Myth of Christian Uniqueness*, 17–18.

6. Panikkar, *The Myth of Christian Uniqueness*, 95.

7. Michael Nazir-Ali, "Embassy, Hospitality and Dialogue: Christians and People of Other Faiths," Lambeth Report 1998. See www.anglicancommunion.org/lambeth/reports/report3.html.

8. Ibid. For a thorough discussion of the "classic" threefold scheme of religious positions — exclusivism, inclusivism, and pluralism — see Robert Davis Hughes III, "Christian Theology of Interfaith Dialogue: Defining the Emerging Fourth Option," *Sewanee Theological Review* 40, no. 4 (1997): 383–408.

9. Peter C. Hodgson, *Revisioning the Church: Ecclesial Freedom in the New Paradigm* (Philadelphia: Fortress, 1988), 94.

10. Michael Ingham, *Mansions of the Spirit: The Gospel in a Multi-Faith World* (Toronto: Anglican Book Centre, 1997), 134. For an alternative point of view, see Lesslie Newbigin, *The Gospel in a Pluralist Society* (Grand Rapids: Wm. B. Eerdmans, 1989), who concludes by accepting *plurality* but rejecting *pluralism* (243–44).

11. Paul Knitter, *Jesus and the Other Names: Christian Mission and Global Responsibility* (Maryknoll, N.Y.: Orbis Books, 1996), 78. See also Frederick R. Wilson, *The San Antonio Report: Your Will Be Done: Mission in Christ's Way*, Commission on World Mission and Evangelism, World Council of Churches (Geneva: WCC Publications, 1990), 32, and David Lochhead, *The Dialogical Imperative: A Christian Reflection on Interfaith Encounter* (Maryknoll, N.Y.: Orbis Books, 1988).

12. Pierre-François de Bethune, O.S.B., *By Faith and Hospitality: The Monastic Tradition as a Model for Interreligious Encounter*, trans. Dame Mary Groves, O.S.B. (Leominster: Gracewing, 2002), 2–3, 18.

13. Esther de Waal, *Living with Contradiction: An Introduction to Benedictine Spirituality* (Harrisburg, Pa.: Morehouse, 1989), from the preface.

Chapter 3: Fireweed Evangelism

1. W. Paul Jones, *Theological Worlds: Understanding the Alternative Rhythms of Christian Belief* (Nashville: Abingdon Press, 1989), 17.

2. Frederick Buechner, "The Dwarves in the Stable," in *Listening for God: Contemporary Literature and the Life of Faith*, ed. Paula J. Carlson and Peter S. Hawkins (Minneapolis: Augsburg Fortress, 1994), 54.

3. Andrew Sung Park, *The Wounded Heart of God: The Asian Concept of Han and the Christian Doctrine of Sin* (Nashville: Abingdon Press, 1993), 10, 76, 73.

4. Henri J. M. Nouwen, *The Wounded Healer* (New York: Doubleday, 1979), 88.

Chapter 5: Backyard Evangelism

1. The 2001 edition of the *Yearbook of American and Canadian Churches* states that there are 133,567,039 full communicant or confirmed members of all Christian churches in the United States. Using a broader definition of affiliation known as inclusive membership, there are 151,161,906 members. U.S. census data for

the year 2000 indicates that the population of the United States in that year was 281,400,000. Thus, 47 percent of the population describes itself as a member of a Christian church, while 54 percent consider themselves to have a Christian affiliation. For year 2000 census data see www.census.gov/prod/2001pubs.

2. This poem is widely attributed to St. Teresa of Avila, but according to Brother Bryan Paquette of the Institute of Carmelite Studies Publications, there is no evidence that St. Teresa either wrote or said this.

3. Sue Monk Kidd, *The Dance of the Dissident Daughter* (San Francisco: HarperSanFrancisco, 1996), 50.

4. George G. Hunter III, *The Celtic Way of Evangelism: How Christianity Can Reach the West . . . Again* (Nashville: Abingdon Press, 2000), 13, 81.

5. Carl S. Dudley and David A. Roozen, *Faith Communities Today: A Report on Religion in the United States Today* (Hartford, Conn.: Hartford Institute for Religion Research, Hartford Seminary, 2001), 15. This comprehensive sixty-eight-page report can be ordered by calling 860-509-9543 or by e-mailing FACT@hartsem.edu. See also http://fact.hartsem.edu/Final%20FACTrpt.pdf.

Chapter 6: Heritage

1. Sue Monk Kidd, *Secret Life of Bees* (New York: Viking, 2002), 107.

2. Walter Brueggemann, *Biblical Perspectives on Evangelism: Living in a Three-Storied Universe* (Nashville: Abingdon Press, 1993), 10.

3. Ibid., 20ff.

4. Klara Tammany, *Living Water: Baptism as a Way of Life* (New York: Church Publishing, 2002). For more information on these programs, see www.alphana.org and www.everyvoice.net. For an excellent "how-to" resource for evangelism and hospitality programs, see www.elca.org/eteam/resources/ResourceLibrary.htm on the web page of the Evangelical Lutheran Church in America.

5. Carl S. Dudley and David A. Roozen, *Faith Communities Today: A Report on Religion in the United States Today* (Hartford, Conn.: Hartford Institute for Religion Research, Hartford Seminary, 2001), 16.

6. Louis R. Jones, *Evangelism in the African American Community: An Evangelism Tool for Today's Church* (New York: Universe, 2003), 11–15.

7. Ibid., 32, 37.

8. Manuel Ortiz, *The Hispanic Challenge: Opportunities Confronting the Church* (Downers Grove, Ill.: InterVarsity Press, 1993), 25–26. Statistics from the U.S. Census Bureau Report for 2002 are obtainable on the Internet.

9. Ortiz, *The Hispanic Challenge*, 61–63, 117–19.

10. Manuel Ortiz, *One New People: Models for Developing a Multiethnic Church* (Downers Grove, Ill.: InterVarsity Press, 1996).

Chapter 7: Vision

1. Carl S. Dudley and David A. Roozen, *Faith Communities Today: A Report on Religion in the United States Today* (Hartford, Conn.: Hartford Institute for Religion Research, Hartford Seminary, 2001), 20.

2. Ibid., 27.

3. The Rev. Sam Leonard, Alban Institute Consultant, A Passion for Lay Ministry Workshop, March 2002. These statistics are based on his research and are used here with permission.

4. Quoted in Robert McAfee Brown, *Unexpected News: Reading the Bible with Third World Eyes* (Philadelphia: Westminster Press, 1984), 98–99.

5. Ibid., 67.

6. Dominique Lapierre, *The City of Joy* (New York: Doubleday, 1985), 40.

7. Quoted in Ann Elizabeth Proctor McElligott, *Evangelism with the Poor: Leader's Guide* (New York: Episcopal Church Center, 1990), 33.

8. Thomas W. Ogletree, *Hospitality to the Stranger: Dimensions of Moral Understanding* (Philadelphia: Fortress Press, 1985), 3–4.

9. Henri J. M. Nouwen, *Reaching Out: The Three Movements of the Spiritual Life* (New York: Doubleday, 1975), 86.

10. Eduard Schweizer, *The Good News According to Matthew* (Atlanta: John Knox Press, 1975), 532.

11. Ibid.

12. Titus Presler, *Horizons of Mission* (Boston: Cowley Publications, 2001), 126–27.

13. Alice Mann, *Incorporation of New Members in the Episcopal Church: A Manual for Clergy and Lay Leaders* (New York: Ascension Press, 1983), 21.

14. Claude E. Payne and Hamilton Beazley, *Reclaiming the Great Commission: A Practical Model for Transforming Denominations and Congregations* (San Francisco: Jossey-Bass, 2000), 19.

15. Bruce Bugbee, Don Cousins, and Bill Hybels, *Network: The Right People ... In the Right Places ... For the Right Reasons — Leader's Guide* (Grand Rapids: Zondervan, 1994), 46, 100, 187. To understand this model, it is important to order the comprehensive video program that contains a videocassette, overheads, a leader's guide and participants' guides, not just the books. All available from Zondervan Publishers.

Chapter 8: Moral Commitment

1. Carl S. Dudley and David A. Roozen, *Faith Communities Today: A Report on Religion in the United States Today* (Hartford, Conn.: Hartford Institute for Religion Research, Hartford Seminary, 2001), 22.

2. William Sloane Coffin, *A Passion for the Members in the Episcopal Church: A* (Louisville: John Knox Press, 1993), 46–47.   : Ascension Press, 1983), 21.

, 40.

Chapter 9: Hospitality Evangelism   7.

1. John Koenig, *New Testament Hospitality: Par* 35–36. *and Mission* (Philadelphia: Fortress Press, 1985), 1 this book for a thorough, in-depth discussion of hos ch, Plainfield, New Jersey, devel- See also Amos 9:13–15; Joel 3:18; and early extrab blet during a presentation of this Testament of Levi 18:11; 1 Enoch 62:14; and Midr:

2. James M. Brice, *I Had a Real Good Time: Th* Reproduced by kind permission ed. Rebel C. Forrester and Betty B. Wood (Union City Publ., 1984), 59.

3. Leonard Swidler, *Biblical Affirmations of Woman* Press, 1979), 183–85.

4. Koenig, *New Testament Hospitality,* 99.

5. Mary Sammons Patton, *Hearts Birds Freed: (* (Princeton, N.J.: Patton Family, 1992), 13.

6. Howard W. Stone, *The Word of God and Pastoral Ca* Press, 1988), 57.

7. Margaret Guenther, *Holy Listening: The Art of Spir* Cowley Publications, 1992), 10.

8. Henri Nouwen, *Reaching Out: The Three Movemen* (New York: Doubleday, 1975), 86.

9. Koenig, *New Testament Hospitality,* 8.

Chapter 10: Components of Successful Hospital

1. Keith Brown, "Congregational Sizes and Characteristi the CODE Conference, San Diego, California, April 2004.

2. Alice Mann, *Raising the Roof: The Pastoral-to-Progra* (Washington, D.C.: Alban Institute, 2001).

3. Marjorie A. Burke, Elizabeth R. Geitz, and Ann Smith *Uncommon Prayers: Our Lives Revealed, Nurtured, Celebrated (* Morehouse, 2000), 362. Prayer written by Ms. Valecia Harriman.

4. Arlin J. Rothauge, *Sizing Up a Congregation for New Member* York: Episcopal Church Center, n.d.), 19.

5. Michael K. Deaver with Mickey Herskowitz, *Behind the Scen* William Morrow and Co., 1987), 82–83. Reprinted with permission Howard Hanchey, *Church Growth and the Power of Evangelism: Idea* (Boston: Cowley Publications, 1990), 113–14.